# THIS LIFE IS GHETTO.

*A Candid Conversation Between a Father and Adult Daughter Navigating Rejection, Divorce and Daddy Issues*

**ASHLEY R WOOD & LEWIS E WOOD**

FOREWORD BY DR TAVIS C TAYLOR

# ABOUT THAT LIFE...

"A lot of us have hurt because we were raised by imperfect parents. And in these pages, you get to listen in on a very unique conversation between a woman who feels the sting of those hurts and the imperfect father who confesses that he failed her. The Woods' story will give you compassion both for those whose actions have hurt the ones they love and also for those who've been hurt. And I pray that it will inspire you to face the loss in your own story so that you might also find the courage to pursue healing and forgiveness."

– **MARGOT STARBUCK**, author of *The Girl in the Orange Dress: Searching for a Father Who Does Not Fail*

"This transparent wounded healer book is a must read by anyone seeking to be transformed through the 'wide open stories' and journey of Ashley (daughter) and Mr. Wood (Poppa dad). They boldly, but humbly share the truths and tragedies, triumphs and trials, and the tests and testimonies of their life story. They are freed from being 'silent sufferers.'

– **DR. KENT BRANCH**, Iron Sharpens Iron Alliance, Author, Businessman, Pastor, Executive Leader

"This Life is Ghetto is a phenomenal book that gives a behind the scenes look into the complexities of families and children that have to deal with divorce and the trauma that can stem from it. The authors remarkably inspire the reader to be honest and vulnerable about the pain that can come from a broken family, and how sometimes, as long as you put in the necessary work, the sins of the father don't have to have the final say, but healing and deliverance can also come from it."

– **DARRION SOMERVILLE**, Pastor, Professor and Veteran

"Ashley Wood delivers a compelling narrative that intricately weaves two distinct perspectives into a unified journey of heartache, self-awareness, reconciliation and ultimate redemption. It's not often that we get such a genuine exploration of the complexities of a father-daughter relationship, depicted here with such raw honesty and sensitivity. Yes, we know they exist but never have we seen it documented like this. The shared narrative invites the reader into a complex dance of love, loss, frustration and resilience, offering a powerful exploration of how family dynamics shape and mold us. I give this book a standing ovation."

– **DR. MARQUISE GOLD**, Marquis Boone Enterprises, Business Executive, author of *Crippled Kings*

"Standing ovation! Thank you for starting this conversation so that many others can begin and continue their own! May God utilize this as an instrument of forgiveness, healing, and transformation for the thousands who don't know where to start and/or why, who, and how to forgive. Lewis offers the gift of a father who was willing to turn around, assess, evaluate, process his life and life choices and gift his daughter with an understanding of unexplainable behavior!"

— **Kelli G. Wood**, Licensed Clinical Social Worker (LCSW), Professor, Pastor, author of *Hiding Place: Overcoming Fear in the Presence of God*

"The honesty and vulnerability shared between a daughter and her father is the type of discussion we need to ignite healing into our families, particularly the African American family. This book sheds light on so many levels that often feel too sacred to explore. I highly recommend this read to those who are in search of parental/child reconciliation."

— **Curnesia S. Bogans**, Licensed Marriage and Family Therapist (LMFT)

"Sticks and stones will break my bones, but words will never hurt. That is a lie from the pit of hell. Words, or the lack thereof, can cause major trauma, unforgiveness, as well as anger. This book is the real life journey between a daughter and her father and the power of words. Communication is imperative when dealing with any transition in life. When words are missing during transition your mind will fill in the blanks with incorrect verbiage. This book must be shared with people who are struggling to forgive. It must be shared with people who are angry at their parents. It must be shared with people who are struggling as adults due to their childhood. Thank you to Ashley and Lewis for helping us on our healing journey."

— **Sonya T. Cruel**, Licensed Clinical Social Worker (LCSW), Transition Coach, Ordained Elder, author of *Divorce in the Upper Room*

ASHLEY R. WOOD & LEWIS E. WOOD

*"As a black father, and a son of divorced military parents, This Life is Ghetto has given me tremendous familiarity of the trials, pain and curiosity we often suffer from as byproducts of parents navigating their own lives. Admittedly so, it has also opened the door of forgiveness and healing for me to enter and explore!"*

— **Michael Danners**, Visual Artist at Iameye Photos

Copyright © 2023 by Ashley R Wood and Lewis E Wood

All rights reserved.

This book or parts thereof may not be reproduced in any form, stored in a retrieval system, or transmitted in any form by any means—electronic, mechanical, photocopy, recording, or otherwise—without prior written permission of the publisher, except as provided by United States of America copyright law.

Visit the authors' website at: www.thislifeisghetto.com.

FIRST EDITION

ISBN: 979-8-9887518-0-9 (paperback)

ISBN: 979-8-9887518-1-6 (ebook)

ISBN: 979-8-9887518-2-3 (epub)

ISBN: 979-8-9887518-3-0 (audio)

Library of Congress Control Number: 2023913680

While the author has made every effort to provide accurate internet addresses at the time of publication, neither the publisher nor the author assumes any responsibility for errors or for changes that occur after publication. Further, the publisher does not have any control over and does not assume any responsibility for the authors or third-party websites or their content.

Printed in the UNITED STATES OF AMERICA

*All photographs courtesy of the authors.*

*Front and back cover design by Michael Danners of Iameye Photos.*

# DEDICATION

This book is dedicated to my parents, Lewis Wood and Carol Sherard. I am who I am today because of you.

*"Honor your father and your mother, as the LORD your God commanded you, that your days may be long, and that it may go well with you in the land that the LORD your God is giving you." ~ Deuteronomy 5:16 (ESV)*

# Contents

| | |
|---|---|
| Foreword | XI |
| PART ONE: The Introduction | 1 |
| 1. Meet the Family | 5 |
| PART TWO: My Father's Story | 36 |
| 2. An Unstable Foundation | 39 |
| 3. The Conversation Starter | 53 |
| PART THREE: Our Story | 65 |
| 4. The Separation | 67 |
| 5. The Reconciliation | 79 |
| 6. The Divorce | 89 |
| 7. Damage of the Spoken and Unspoken | 97 |
| 8. Collateral Damage | 105 |
| PART FOUR: Our Healing Continues | 122 |
| 9. What We Should Have Said | 123 |
| 10. Forgiveness and Healing | 127 |

| | |
|---|---|
| 11. A Letter to the Daughter | 135 |
| 12. Letters to the Father | 137 |
| Our Parting Words | 141 |
| Acknowledgments | 143 |
| About the Authors | 150 |

# Foreword

In the pages that follow, you will embark on a profound journey—a candid conversation that transcends the boundaries of generational gaps, deep-seated resentments, and the complexities of human relationships. *This Life is Ghetto: A Candid Conversation Between a Father and Adult Daughter: Navigating Rejection, Divorce, and Daddy Issues* is an extraordinary memoir, co-authored by Ashley Wood and her father, Lewis Wood. This compelling narrative delves into the intricate web of emotions and experiences that have shaped their lives, offering a poignant exploration of forgiveness, redemption, and the power of love.

Theirs is a story of shattered trust, heartache, and the arduous path toward healing. Ashley, once burdened with resentment toward her father, shares her vulnerability, unveiling the layers of pain and confusion that haunted her for years. Growing up in the shadow of her father's vocation as a preacher, Ashley experienced the weight of societal expectations and the struggle to live up to the idealized image of a preacher's child. But beneath the surface of her resentment lies a profound longing for understanding and reconciliation.

Lewis, a man whose actions tore his family apart, seizes this opportunity to shed light on his own journey of self-discovery and redemption. As he reflects on the choices he made, the pain he inflicted, and the consequences he faced, Lewis bares his soul with unflinching honesty. Through his narrative, he unveils the complexities of human nature, the fallibility of our choices, and the enduring strength of the bond between father and daughter.

Their shared story transcends the boundaries of personal experience, offering a glimpse into the universal struggles that many individuals face within their own families. It touches upon themes of forgiveness, healing, and the power of introspection. Through their raw and intimate conversations, Ashley and Lewis invite us to examine our own relationships, to confront the pain and resentment that may reside within, and to find the courage to embark on our own journeys of healing and growth.

This book is not merely an account of past events, but a living testament to the transformative power of empathy, understanding, and forgiveness. It serves as a reminder that, despite the trials and tribulations we face in our relationships, there is always hope for redemption and reconciliation. It is a beacon of light that guides us toward a path of healing, not just for Ashley and Lewis, but for all those who have experienced the pain of fractured familial bonds.

As you immerse yourself in the profound conversations between Ashley and Lewis, may their words resonate deeply within your heart. May this extraordinary journey serve as an inspiration for you to confront your own demons, to embrace forgiveness and understanding, and to strive for healing within your own relationships. Together, let us embark on this transformative odyssey—a testament to the enduring power of love, forgiveness, and the unbreakable bond between a father and his daughter.

Acknowledging the complexities and sensitivities of the topics explored within these pages, it is essential to approach this candid conversation with empathy and an open mind. Ashley and Lewis have bravely chosen to share their deeply personal narratives, baring their souls, in an effort to foster understanding and promote healing. Their willingness to engage in this dialogue serves as a testament to the power of vulnerability and the profound impact it can have on our lives.

Through their words, we are reminded that no relationship is immune to trials and tribulations. The bond between a father and daughter, once seen as unbreakable, can be tested and strained by the complexities of human nature. The emotional scars left by rejection, divorce, and unresolved "daddy issues" can create a chasm that seems insurmountable. However, Ashley and Lewis demonstrate that, with compassion, introspection, and a willingness to engage in open and honest communication, bridges can be built, wounds can heal, and forgiveness can flourish.

In the following chapters, you will witness the transformation of a fractured relationship—a metamorphosis guided by introspection, understanding, and a shared desire for reconciliation. Ashley's journey from resentment to forgiveness is a testament to the power of compassion and the strength that lies within the human spirit. Lewis, too, embarks on a path of self-reflection, confronting the consequences of his actions and seeking redemption.

As you immerse yourself in the stories shared by Ashley and Lewis, it is my hope that you will find solace, inspiration, and a renewed sense of faith in the power of healing. This conversation serves as a reminder that, no matter how deep the wounds may be, no matter how insurmountable the obstacles may seem, there is always a glimmer of hope—a chance for growth, understanding, and the restoration of a fractured bond.

We live in a world where forgiveness is often seen as weakness, and the scars of past hurts can overshadow the potential for healing. Yet, Ashley and Lewis challenge these notions, inviting us to examine our own relationships and confront the pain that may reside within. They remind us that the path to healing begins with acknowledging our own vulnerabilities, embracing empathy, and daring to engage in candid conversations that foster understanding and compassion.

As you embark on this poignant journey, I encourage you to approach these pages with an open heart and a willingness to reflect upon your own experiences. Allow the shared experiences of Ashley and Lewis to ignite conversations within your own life, bridging divides and fostering a greater sense of connection with those you hold dear.

May *This Life is Ghetto: A Candid Conversation Between a Father and Adult Daughter: Navigating Rejection, Divorce, and Daddy Issues* serve as a catalyst for healing, understanding, and ultimately, the restoration of fractured relationships. May it remind us all of the power of forgiveness and the profound impact that love and compassion can have on our lives.

THIS LIFE IS GHETTO.

Dr. Tavis C. Taylor,

Certified Christian Counselor and Anger Management Coach. Author, *The Science of Positive Neuropsychology*. Business Strategist, Mom, **Daddy's Girl**

## PART ONE: The Introduction

*"You may not control all the events that happen to you, but you can decide not to be reduced by them." ~ Maya Angelou*

\*\*\*

You may have heard or articulated one or more of the following: *Adulting is ghetto. Adulting is overrated. Parenting is ghetto. Life be life-ing.* These are just a few urban colloquialisms that can become more accurate and relatable the older we get, which brings us here and to why I am transparently sharing my story.

I began writing this book as an act of obedience. God instructed me to share how life has been life-ing and how He's helped me navigate it. Without Him, I would be an extra, reheated hot mess. So here we are. Would I have rather shared my experiences another way? Absolutely. But I do know the positive impact will far outweigh any shame or apprehension I may have had.

I'm not sure what has drawn you here, but I thank you for joining the journey. To the daughter who has ever felt rejected by her father, this book is for you. To the daughter who is struggling with or has struggled with daddy issues, this book is for you. To the adult son or adult daughter who has witnessed and experienced the divorce of their parents, this book is also for you. To the adult child who is still battling unforgiveness and hoarding resentment toward a parent, this book is definitely for you.

Over the last two years, I have been intentional about rediscovering myself. I have been intentional about conducting a full inventory of my heart and clearing out hidden resentment. I've gone to therapy and done the hard work of peeling off layers and layers of emotional trigger points. And the work is still in action.

I invited my father along for the ride. For Part I of the *This Life is Ghetto.* series, we focus on the full-circle healing and repair of our relationship. Our father-daughter dynamic has been an interesting rollercoaster ride. We often only hear about the wreckage of daddy issues. Rarely do we hear about the reconciliation and repair that can happen. Some of you may know this world well. The breakdown in our relationship initially stemmed from my father's insecurities as a man. Understandably, my dad could not quite grasp what it took to be a responsible husband and father. The foundation was unstable. The domino effect was in motion. Then, the dissolution of his marriage to my mom continued the breakdown of our relationship.

My parents first separated when I was eighteen, got back together in my mid-twenties, separated again when I was thirty-two, and officially divorced right before I turned thirty-three. Ghetto, right? And because of *how* my father left both times, I struggled with separating who he was as my father from who he was as my mother's husband. Unknowingly, I lumped them together because of my innocent ignorance.

Now that I am on the other side of the madness, I pray my story will help others. Even you. After I introduce you to the family, the remaining chapters will give you a front row seat to our candid conversation. You won't leave disappointed. You will learn more about who I am. You will learn more about my father. You will capture the human side of who he is apart from society's labels.

If you know us personally, whether as family, friend, foe, acquaintance, hater, coworker, church member, or nosey bystander, some details of this book may take you aback, surprise you, and make you rethink what you thought you knew. And that's ok. It is important to remember that we are all flawed humans trying to figure out life and keep our sanity while doing so. There are many of you out there with a similar story. You're struggling with the same emotions and trying not to repeat the ever-growing cycle of broken relationships with a parent or guardian. For those who cannot relate, there is still something for you, too.

You may be wondering why I categorized this life as *ghetto*. Historically, the word has had a negative connotation, especially in the Black community. But when handled recklessly, life can be "makeshift, shoddy, or left in a poor condition," according to the *Oxford English Dictionary*. When *ghetto* is used as a verb, it means to "put in or restrict to an isolated or segregated area or group." Well, that's exactly what rejection, daddy issues, and divorced parents can do to you. They can *ghetto* you (Yep, I made that up!) and isolate you in ways you didn't sign up for or are ready to face.

As Dr. Tavis Taylor stated in the foreword, this is a journey. I begin by discussing the background details of my immediate family. I believe knowing the characters and their personalities will help you understand more about who I am and why I've never given up. It will also establish the context for the conversation I had with my father.

In Part Two, my dad shares more about his childhood and how his unstable foundation started as a man and a father. Part Three reflects our individual perspectives around a similar timeline of events leading up to my parents' divorce. In Part Three, we also share how damaging the unspoken can be in relationships, while highlighting the beauty and life lessons of the collateral damage. Part Four provides our thoughts on healing and forgiveness to assist you in your own forgiveness journey. Lastly, we close it out with parting thoughts to each other as father and daughter.

I pray our transparency opens your eyes to the levels of hurt, damage, disappointment, retrospect, and even the healing that can ensue if you receive it. I pray your mind and heart are open to different perspectives outside of your own. I pray you have or can forgive your parent(s) for what they did or did not do. I pray you forgive them for not having a manual handed to them on how to rear the human(s) God entrusted to them. And I pray you forgive yourself for all the dumb and stupid choices you made as a result. For those who have given up hope, I pray you try again. The grace we all desire to receive from others is the same grace we should dish out. Trust me, I know firsthand.

# 1

## Meet the Family

Let's kick this thing off with a personal introduction. I am Ashley Rebecca, a one-of-a-kind human being. My beautiful maternal grandmother named me. It was between "Ashley" and "Leah," which was an option my mom had for me. I entered this world a solid eight pounds and some change, with a big head and wide hips!

I was born in Atlanta, GA, and reared in Stone Mountain, a city east of Atlanta. According to doctors and science, I should not be here, but clearly God had another plan. I come from a strong extended family unit where you had to grow thick skin. We love hard in our own unique way without the mush. I am the youngest and have three older brothers. I definitely broke the stereotype of being a spoiled brat as the baby and only girl. It would have been a waste of time, energy, and expectations. I identified and respected that my parents did not have money to spoil me like they wanted to as I was growing up.

We lived in a middle-class neighborhood, but I never quite saw us as middle class. Once I was old enough to understand, there always seemed to be some level of struggle. And most of it was financially based. I didn't always have what I wanted, but at a minimum, I had what I needed. Up until I was four years old, my parents had to move around a lot from place to place. We finally stopped moving once I was in kindergarten. This established a sense of stability and relief. Just my youngest brother and I were left in the house at this point. My oldest brother was in Boston, and my middle brother was away at college.

Before we moved into the house I consider my childhood home, my parents were put into an unfortunate situation. The owners of our old house had defaulted on the loan and had not been paying the mortgage. The rent my parents paid each month was being applied elsewhere. Trifling. My parents found out when the marshals came knocking at the door one day. We were given about two weeks to move out. There was not much time to process the urgency. Even as a four-year-old, it was hard to leave because I loved that house. I was sad that we had to abruptly move. But I was relieved when I heard we had somewhere to go.

We lived in the next house, in Stone Mountain, until the summer before my sophomore year of college. This was a big deal because my brothers had experienced a lot of house moves and school changes. As a result, they thought I had "the good life" compared to theirs.

But my life in that household was one of survival. It was where I learned how to be a problem solver and a critical thinker. I learned not to wait for things to be handed to me. I would often hear, "You gotta learn to figure it out." I am the same way now, and I love to troubleshoot. I also have a knack for organizing and making small spaces work to my advantage. I prefer to find a solution rather than sit and complain. Complaining is a major pet peeve for me. I picked up many things by merely watching and observing. There was not a lot of opportunity for hands-on training. This was and still is one of the benefits of being the youngest.

When I was in the fourth grade, my mom had to have major surgery. Leading up to the surgery, she gave me a crash course on personal responsibility. I was already a latchkey kid, like my brothers. This was when neighborhoods were safer, and all the neighbors knew each other by name. She had to make sure I was good once I got home from school and while my dad was at work at the fire house. I felt so mature once I got my own house key. I quickly learned how to sort and wash clothes, iron, and how to properly and safely clean by myself. I also learned how to curl my hair and keep it maintained. Oddly enough, she wouldn't let me use the stove without supervision. She later shared that she had been burned by fish grease as a child. She still has discoloration from the burn on her face. That memory never left her, and she has always been overly protective of small children in the kitchen.

Since the age nine, I have valued being self-sufficient. With this self-sufficiency came a necessary reliance on God. My mom always taught me that I had to know God for myself because I wouldn't be able to always rely on them. To this day, she emphasizes the importance of prayer and the fruit it yields. As a child, church was a memorable and major part of my life.

My dad began pastoring a small church in South Georgia right before I was born. When I was seven, he became the pastor of a church in Atlanta where he pastored for five years. Thankfully, my mom ensured we had a balance between our church life and personal life. My great aunt, who I affectionately call "Auntie Grandma," lived near the church, and we could escape there.

My childhood church was my training ground for serving and public speaking. It was where I learned to think on my feet quickly and to always be ready to be called upon. I could sit down in the pew, ready for a three o'clock in the afternoon service, and discover that my name was on the program for a welcome, song, etc. Church was where I was pretty much in every auxiliary or ministry. I was a junior usher and a regular usher. I sang in the children's and adult choirs, I helped clean up on Saturdays, I led devotion, and I helped my mom print and fold programs. Since my dad was the pastor, if no one showed up or if there was a gap, one of us filled in and kept it moving. Again, we lived by the mantra: "You gotta learn to figure it out."

Church is where I learned to watch and cover those in authority. I was probably my mom's first armorbearer. Church is where I learned to sit for long periods of time and act like I had some sense. *If you know, you know.* Church was comedy, and there rarely was a dull moment. Today's generation wouldn't even understand.

Church is where I learned that adults put on a façade to mask the truth. Some in high positions or with titles had real life struggles they worked hard to keep hidden. Others who disliked, disrespected, or even hated my parents were the same ones who would smile in my face, as if I was oblivious to the buffoonery. You couldn't love me and hate my parents. The two didn't mix.

However, church is where I learned about community and how to develop relationships. Church is where I met some good, solid folks who I still love and cherish. The church is where I became more observant of people and interested in how and why they moved the way they did.

*** 

I have always been a realist, and it never took a lot to please me. I love the simple things. Birthdays were always celebrated with my extended family, mainly on my mom's side. The majority of the time, birthday parties were spent at Auntie Grandma's house, my grandma's baby sister. Even before my grandma passed, she treated me like a granddaughter, not just a great-niece. The birthday menu was always simple and easy: hotdogs, hamburgers, chips, and Little Hugs Fruit Barrels aka "hug n jugs." We would even have ribs sometimes. You had to be a certain age to drink soda. Dessert would be a birthday cake with a gallon tub of vanilla or Neapolitan (aka Napoleon) ice cream. Throw in a game of spades and bid whist, with some good music, and you had yourself a party.

For holidays, we would either be at Auntie Grandma's house or drive to South Carolina. We would host every now and then, or my cousin, Auntie Grandma's daughter, would host at her house. But I always looked forward to visiting the country. I loved to sit on the front porch and wave at folks as they drove by.

When Christmas season rolled around, I would pull out the Christmas ads from the $0.75 Sunday newspaper, circle my top three to five choices, and leave it on the kitchen counter. That way, my parents (really my mama) didn't have to guess what I wanted. I did this faithfully. Nine times out of ten, I would get exactly what I requested. Even if it was only one of my choices.

If my dad had to work at the firehouse on Christmas Day, we would open his gifts the day before. Christmas Eve was also typically the day my mom was able to purchase all the gifts and wrap them in enough time.

My favorite dolls were Barbie and Cabbage Patch Kids. When the Cabbage Patch Kids Pretty Crimp N Curl Doll came out, you would have thought I was a licensed cosmetologist. I would crimp and spiral that baby's hair to perfection. I always wanted an American Girl doll, but my parents couldn't afford one. I appreciated when my mom would order the magazines for me, so I could stay up-to-date on the models.

My toy collection was balanced, though. I had G.I. Joe toys and race cars. I had a green Hess toy truck that I absolutely loved. Don't ask me why. I was so sad when my mom made me give it away to a cousin. I don't even remember who got the truck for me.

***

I also used to be bashful and dreaded speaking in front of people. It felt like torture, and it was a major fear. I mean, I would cry if I was asked or forced to speak at church. Asking me to sing was even worse. My mom would give me that look which meant *do not embarrass me.* Some of you know that look very well. Whoever would call me up had more confidence in me than I had in myself. Looking down to avoid eye contact rarely worked.

Oddly enough, I was not bashful at school. I guess it was because I didn't have the glaring eyes of adults on me, only kids my age with a sprinkle of adult teachers. The church adults were supportive, but I only wanted their support from the pew and out of the spotlight.

My first memorable debut was my role as a crying pig in a school play. I was in kindergarten. I don't remember what the play was about, but it involved farm animals. My mom made me this dope, pink pig outfit with a tail. I think I still have it somewhere in storage. I snagged a free pig nose from a McDonald's Happy Meal. The line I had was "Boo-hoo! Boo-hoo!"

Each time my character was up to speak, this is all I had to remember. The teacher had me fake some tears as I did the crying hand motion over both eyes. My parents told me I had great acting skills as a kid. I could cry at the drop of a hat. I mean, your girl was good.

*The day of Ashley's debut in the school play.*

\*\*\*

Another great memory was learning American Sign Language (ASL) in the first and second grade. I attended a Christian school in Decatur. Along with teaching us ASL fundamentals, my teacher taught us how to sign to gospel songs. Our class would perform at school functions and for the school's Sunday church services. One song I recall is "We Shall Behold Him" by Vickie Winans.

Surprisingly, I was never nervous or felt bashful when we performed. Maybe, I felt more comfortable signing versus speaking out loud. I would zone out and focus on the words of the song. I focused on not messing up, and I appreciated the love we received.

As you can probably guess, I never preferred to be in the spotlight. However, I have never been able to stay under the radar for too long. I am definitely an extrovert by trade and an introvert by choice. But God seems not to care about this personal choice.

I was always considered smart, and academics came easy for me. I stayed on the honor roll. I loved school and learning new things. I valued timeliness and order. And I still do. Both make my soul happy. Cleaning became very therapeutic. I can think clearly when I clean. I loved to see the fresh vacuum lines and hated for anyone to walk over my work of art.

My mom would give my brother and me a list of chores every week. Any chore my brother did not want to do, I would charge him to get it done. Call it entrepreneurship. The price was worth more than hearing our mom fuss when she got home.

My mom says that "I did not fool with a lot of people" and "I liked who I liked." If I didn't care for you, I had a way of looking straight through you. I was sweet and even-tempered until you crossed me. I have never liked nonsense. It was not until third grade that I really felt the need to be vocal and stand up for myself. I went to a predominantly white Christian school for that year only. There were only a few kids I genuinely liked, but I loved my teacher. Most of the kids came off as rude or standoffish.

One day at recess, this kid called me the N-word. I don't know if my parents ever broke down the negativity around that word. However, I *instantly* knew he had disrespected me. I felt a little sad, and I wanted to punch him in his face. I don't remember what I said to him, but I know I went and told a teacher. Sadly, the teacher did nothing but give me some pitiful speech on how the little boy didn't know any better. I went home and told my parents. They tried their best to school me (on a third-grade level) on why it was wrong. I have never forgotten that day and the way it made me feel.

***

Until I hit a tomboy stage in middle school, I was a very particular child who loved clothes and fashion. As a result, my great-aunt Julia would call me "Nancy Reagan." She told my dad he needed to keep a job to support my fashion habit. My mom insisted on dressing me nicely, especially for church.

In those days, you always looked your best for church. It was non-negotiable. I was that kid with the big hair bows, pretty tulle dresses with the matching purse, ruffled socks, and shiny black patent leather shoes.

My mom always wanted for me to look pretty and for my hair to be done. The reason was because she never wanted for me to feel less than, and because of this, I saw a tangible reflection of my worth, with a strong emphasis on never feeling less than.

When my mom was a little girl, she had nice clothes, but she didn't always feel good enough. Her outward appearance, sometimes, didn't align with how she felt inside. Fortunately, I never felt less than as a little girl. I always felt like I was more than enough. Family members tell stories about how I would walk around like I was cute and you couldn't tell me anything. Some described me as snooty.

But I thank my mom for this confidence. I thank her for encouraging me to value my appearance. I also wanted to be a model. A family friend nicknamed me "Vanna Black" (the black version of Vanna White from *Wheel of Fortune*). I would critique people's outfits and call it out if a woman's purse didn't match her shoes. It's okay. You're allowed to judge me for two seconds.

In addition to my modeling aspirations, I wanted to be a writer. *It's crazy how I've literally come full circle.* As a young girl, I would crawl into a tiny spot in my bedroom closet. This was my office where I'd perfect my penmanship and spelling skills by writing up newspapers and store ads. I don't know how or why I started doing this, but I would copy words and sentences until there was no free space left in the advertisements or my composition books. This is probably why I am now the go-to proofreader and can always point out a misspelled word or typo. I learned calligraphy after someone gifted me with a set. As a result, I also love a good writing pen. Sharpie pens are my favorite.

In that same closet, I would imagine who and what I would become without reservation. I knew no fear. I had the biggest faith and would always dream big. I would dream big about my career ambitions. Once I realized my love for writing, I informed my fifth-grade teacher. Throughout the school year, she gave me intentional feedback on my writing assignments. She encouraged me and planted a seed that is now flourishing. If only I could find her and tell her thank you.

I would also talk to God and pray for others in this closet. At church, we had a "sick and shut-in" list for those who couldn't make it to church.

There was also a bereaved list for members who had a death in their family. I would take the back of the church program and call out their names in prayer. I can recall my mother instructing me to pray for a family member or family friend on occasion. I would write down their name on a piece of paper and intercede for them. I knew God heard and answered my prayers. This closet was my safe space. My faith-filled space. Another place where I could think clearly. My fearless space.

***

Around fourth and fifth grade, I finally started learning R&B and hip-hop songs. This probably sounds odd or funny to some of you. Don't judge. I went to a Christian school up until third grade and lived in the church, so I deserve a pass. Luckily, public school, friends, and family kept me musically and socially balanced. But I grew up on hymns and gospel music. All we bought were gospel cassette tapes. The Winans, Commissioned, Take 6, Mississippi Mass Choir, and John P. Kee were some of my favorites.

I don't remember hearing anything outside of old-school music and gospel in the house. I have always loved all types of music and especially fell in love with Motown at an early age. My parents were also music lovers, but I think they intentionally avoided much of the music from their time for various reasons. My dad usually played smooth jazz and the blues. My mom loved Luther Vandross and Oleta Adams.

After I got my first stereo in either the sixth or seventh grade, I would sneak and listen to V-103 and the Quiet Storm in my room. I knew to turn it down low enough to avoid getting caught. My room was right next to my parents' room. If there was any movement in the hallway, I would turn it all the way down.

I used cassette tapes to record my favorite songs and learn the words. Once side A got full, I would flip that bad boy over and continue on side B. I also learned how to fade the music out once the end of a song approached. I diversified my tape and CD collection after that.

I was allowed to watch music videos as long as they were not vulgar or didn't have a lot of cursing. But I was tired of being the oddball who only knew *church* and *God stuff*. I was already abnormal because we were at church three to four days out of the week. And don't let it be revival or convention time. That's an easy six days straight, and I still had to get up and go to school. I couldn't go where my friends went. I wasn't allowed to attend sleepovers, and I surely didn't go to everyone's birthday party. A part of me wanted to be, somewhat, relatable to my peers.

Also around sixth grade, I began getting into trouble at school. I think being a pre-teen did it. I had been mannerable and didn't give my folks any grief up until that point. It was always my mouth that got me in trouble. I didn't intend to be disrespectful, but I needed my voice to be heard.

My mom's favorite story to tell is when I flipped over a chair in my math class. The teacher told me to do something I disagreed with, so I flipped the chair over, and I think I dared him to say something. Don't ask how or why I lost my mind at that moment. The teacher and I later made amends, and he was one of my favorite teachers by the end of the school year.

Once I got to seventh grade, it seemed like a teacher called my house every other week. One of them had it out for me. My mom never believed me and thought I was making it up. That was when the teacher's side of the story trumped mine, or the actual account of events. The final straw came when I told the teacher to stop calling my house. I was tired of hearing my mom fuss.

As you can probably guess, I got my butt whooped that evening because the teacher definitely snitched and called my bluff. And I was put on punishment. Later, my brother's old gym teacher vouched for me and said the teacher was messy. It was then, and only then, that my mom started believing me. I owe Coach for that lifeline. I finally leveled out once I got to high school.

I also became a tomboy in seventh grade. It was right after my dad stopped pastoring. One morning, I woke up, and my body had totally changed. Puberty literally hit me overnight. I am not exaggerating. I went to bed one way and woke up another way. The weight gain was a little overwhelming because I had not hit a growth spurt yet. But I must have carried the weight well to other people or they were just trying to be nice. They never believed me when I told them how much I weighed. I remember my science teacher calling attention to my weight gain as I walked into class one morning. She tilted her head a little and said, "You're spreading out there, Ashley." I wanted to clap back and say, "Ya mama!", but I refrained myself.

Thankfully, the classroom had not filled up with my classmates yet. I was so embarrassed and agitated. I became very self-conscious about my body after that. To hide the curves, I would sneak in my brother's closet and take his shirts. They were big enough to cover me up. He eventually caught on. I would ask him for the old jeans he no longer wore. I would throw on an extra-large belt, wrap it around a second time, and keep it moving. I only dressed up and wore girly clothes for church.

My mom hated it, and she could not understand why I wanted to wear my brother's clothes. My desire to wear baggy clothes baffled her altogether. I don't think my brother understood it either. It wasn't totally odd because this was the era of oversized clothes and Starter jackets.

Nonetheless, this was totally contradictory to the image my mom had of her baby girl who loved to dress up. If she saw me before leaving the house for school, she would make me change immediately. I, then, made sure to head to the bus stop in enough time before she woke up. My mom would, sometimes, joke with me about my puberty phase. I never told her what my teacher said. I never shared with her that the jokes reminded me of the embarrassment. I didn't need anyone else calling out my insecurities. We didn't talk about the resentment until I was in my early twenties. But I never told her the full reason.

I was no longer that little girl who felt like I was more than enough. I started to feel less than. How I dressed reflected how I felt. The criticism I received was rarely laced with affirmations to cushion the blows. I was, somewhat, still a tomboy during high school, but it wasn't as extreme. You still wouldn't catch me wearing many dresses or showing a lot of skin. Whenever I wore something fitted that showed my shape, it was an entire spectacle of pure shock and confusion. I mostly heard, "Where have you been hiding that body?" It didn't take long for me to cover up again.

I did not date or have boyfriends in high school. I don't remember ever going through a boy-crazy phase either. I had two distinct boy crushes when I was younger, but we won't call out any names. I thought boys were cute; I just wasn't interested. I was always cooler with them than I was with girls, though. I could count on one hand the number of female friends I had.

In the ninth grade, I got in trouble for trying to see an older boy. Back then, we had house phones. One evening, I was on the phone chatting with the boy, and my parents called to check-in. I left him on hold. Once I was done with my parents, I did not double-click back over to clear out the call.

Consequently, the remainder of my conversation with the boy was recorded on our home voicemail. After my parents heard the voicemail message, they called me back to share their discovery. This was a crappy way of getting caught. Regrettably, it took some time to regain my parents' trust.

My mom was pissed, and my dad was disappointed. Their underlying concern was softened a little once they learned I didn't have sex with him. While relieved, they were still shocked about the sneaking. I'm sure that planted a seed of me *assuming* they would *not allow* me to date after that. I felt I had let them down. Actually, I *knew* I had let them down. I walked on eggshells for a few months. I didn't try sneaking around again, and boys never became a priority. The guilt was too much.

My parents didn't talk to me a lot about dating. They may have told me I had to wait to date until I was sixteen or seventeen. That would be my guesstimate. I know my mom emphasized education and staying focused. Boys would come later. My dad emphasized that boys lied. They would always lie. End of story. So we definitely didn't talk about sex. That was almost taboo.

As Southerners, young ladies were instructed to *keep their pocketbooks closed*. A pocketbook is a type of purse or handbag. It's also a euphemism for the value between our legs. In other words, don't let a boy peek inside to avoid giving in to the temptation.

From my perspective, there was not a lot of conversation around *how* to keep the pocketbook closed. All I heard was that it was a sin to have sex before marriage. My mom came from a very conservative background and household. She didn't get the talk either. Her folks didn't know how to have those types of conversations. They also had to figure it out on their own. So she would jokingly tell me to go ride a bike or take a cold shower if I felt the urge.

My dad raised himself, and he also figured out sex on his own from the streets. He, straight away, avoided any kind of direction or advice around this subject. And we certainly didn't have these conversations in church. So I received my sex education from public school and relationships.

***

As I mentioned earlier, I am the youngest of four children. Although I'm the youngest, I do not play about my siblings. At. All. I will fight you, with the intention of demolishing you with all my might, if you come for them. *No, seriously.* The older we get, the more I'm inclined to protect them for some reason. My oldest brother is Damon, my dad's first son from a prior relationship. We are seventeen years apart. I did not grow up around him since he lived in Boston with his mom, and he was so much older.

He has always had this distinct Cambridge/Boston accent that reminds me of an Ivy League professor. There's a depth to his voice, similar to our dad's, and he has a certain distinguished presence about him. The strained relationship he had with our dad impacted our ability to bond as siblings. Distance had something to do with it as well. He visited more before I was born and when I was really little.

I always desired to have a closer relationship with him as his little sister. There was so much I wanted to learn from him. After our grandmother passed in 2005, he came down for the service. We gathered at my brother's house the night before. It was so good to see all of us joking and laughing together. My brothers and I definitely share a similar sense of humor and sarcasm. Damon looks so much like our dad and grandmother that it's a little scary. He and my sister-in-law made me an aunt for the first time. I remember being so excited when I heard the news.

Damon is an incredible actor and performer. He displays his talents across many stages in the New England area. He has been an understudy for many plays, such as *Fences* and *Joe Turner's Come and Gone*, both by August Wilson. I have a goal to make it up there to see him in action, sooner rather than later. The plane tickets are so high! Looking back, I probably inherited my childhood acting chops from him and didn't even know it.

Next in line is Ronnie. He is my mom's oldest son from her first marriage and is fourteen years older than me. Ronnie is a protector. He often keeps tabs on me and my travels. My sister-in-law has to remind him often that

I'm grown. He is a confidant and a comedian, and his word is bond. Ronnie is also a man of few words. He drops the best life nuggets in everyday conversations. You gotta pay attention to catch them. He is legit one of my favorite people in the entire world. He taught me how to read and never tortured me like the other brother you'll meet soon. Word on the street is I would only listen to him when I was younger because I thought everyone else was dumb or didn't know anything.

Because of my and Ronnie's age gap, my early memories were of him being away at Florida A&M University (FAMU). I would always get excited when he would come home to visit. Up until my senior year of high school, I was going to FAMU because of him. (Well, they were slow on sending my acceptance letter. It didn't arrive until late that summer after I graduated.) So I went with the best decision I could have made and enrolled at Tuskegee University.

But Ronnie gave me the best advice before I left for college that I have never forgotten — "Don't be a ho. Don't get pregnant. Graduate on time." It was memorable because it came from him. His statement didn't add any context to sex or dating from what I had not received from my parents. But it still served as a compass for college life. Fortunately, I was able to accomplish all three directives.

Ronnie also taught me to be a go-getter. He paved the way for me and my brother Lathan. Once Ronnie left home for college, he made it his business to figure out life. He had no choice. My parents could not provide him with everything he needed. He worked, had fun, and took on responsibilities during undergrad and even afterward. He has always emphasized the importance of being a great steward of your finances. I doubt that you will ever catch him without money. He's wise in so many areas, which makes him great for giving advice.

But I caution—do not ask him for advice or his opinion, if you're not ready for his response. I also don't recommend wasting the knowledge he shares with you. All it takes is to fumble the ball one time. You can only return once you're truly ready to take action. Since I'm the last one left to get married, he reminds me never to rush it. He also reminds me never to allow others to rush me into motherhood. I will know when the time is right. Ronnie tells me to always know what I want and to be able to articulate it, especially to my companion — "Closed mouths don't get fed. Nobody can read your mind. Always say what you mean and mean what you say."

Next is my "down like four flat tires" brother and duet partner, Lathan. We are five years apart, and we share the same mother and father. He's protective in a more low-key kind of way, always showing up when it means the most. His intellect and musical ingenuity are top-notch. He is a talented producer with an excellent ear. He tends to use big words, so you will need a dictionary and thesaurus nearby when conversing with him.

As with many brothers and sisters, we didn't start this sibling journey on the best of terms. Lathan packed his little suitcase and ran away after I was born. He was headed to our grandmother's house across town for refuge. He also let me fall off a car when I was a baby. He says it was an accident. I think he intentionally dropped me (insert sinister side eye here) because he was mad I took his spot as the youngest.

I couldn't stand to sit next to him in the backseat. I couldn't stand for him to even look at me. Our parents would be so sick of us by the time we got where we were going. Now there was this huge space between us, big enough where you could pull the armrest down to separate us. He would still inch his way over to aggravate me and point his finger toward my eye or ear. Pure torture.

Lathan would also practice his WWE moves on me when my parents left him in charge. He even had the nerve to try out the DDT move on me. The boy had lost his mind. But it toughened me up because I had no choice but to fight back.

We fought. We tore up the house together. We covered it up together. Snitching was not allowed. If one told, both of us got in trouble. Our mom would yell down the steps, "What y'all down there doing?!" Our immediate response in unison would be "Nothing!" without fail, every time. Then, we'd go right back at it.

One of our favorite things to do was to use wrapping paper rolls to hit each other. We would run around in a circle chasing each other until we got tired. If it wasn't cardboard, it was a foil pan. With the foil pan, the ultimate goal was to pop each other smack dab in the middle of the forehead. The placement of the hit was significant to achieve a particular sound. We would run around throwing cups of water at each other, wetting up the kitchen walls and cabinets. Luckily, we would successfully clean up the mess in enough time. Great times.

We also suffered long church days together. We constructed some of the best struggle meals, including delicious fried bologna sandwiches with homemade fries, together. He is the reason why I love condiments, hot sauce, and practically any other kind of sauce on my food.

Lathan taught me to go with the flow and to be a risk-taker. Ronnie and I are very methodical, while Lathan is adventurous and fearless. He's a visionary like our dad. Lathan is also the top jokester. If the three of us get together, it is a wrap, ladies and gentlemen. We can cut all the way up. While Lathan can never hold his laughter, I'm in the middle, trying to be the mature one, and Ronnie sits there, straight-faced, as if he didn't instigate the shenanigans.

Lathan also taught me how to drive with my knee. He taught me that efficient multi-tasking is essential as a driver. I practiced my left turns with him. He would judge me if it wasn't smooth enough. "Sister, that left turn still needs work." He is a true salesman and will have you buying a hammer in a music store if you let him. My brother, Lathan, is an agitator in the best way. If you're not operating at your highest potential, he will call you out on it.

***

Last, but certainly not least, are my parents, Lewis and Carol. My parents were my first introductions to forging a personal relationship with God. I grew up a "preacher's kid" or PK. Both of my parents are ordained elders, and my dad was a pastor in my early years. The PK label was, sometimes, annoying and came with great responsibility. People held me to a higher standard than I did myself most of the time.

I just wanted to be a normal kid. But I couldn't always do what everyone else did. Often, I wouldn't tell people that my parents were preachers. Some would start acting funny or not be themselves around me, as if I would judge them.

My parents did not allow any of us to be mediocre or lazy. My mom would always tell my brothers, "No woman wants a sorry man." They equipped us with the basics, so we could make it in the real world. If we messed up or got in trouble, we automatically knew they would put us on punishment. Punishment, or being grounded, meant no talking on the phone, no going outside, no fraternizing with friends, no fun, and no TV for, at least, one week. We went to school, came home, ate dinner, then looked at the four walls of our room for the rest of the night.

Picture hearing and watching our friends playing and having fun outside. And all I could do was crack the shade a little and peek out my bedroom window with envy. They would just wave and laugh if they caught me peeking. So embarrassing. Or I went to church and was silent. I had to whisper or pass a note to my friends, letting them know that I couldn't talk. Kids today could never!

As the only girl, they both made it clear that the rulebook changed with me. Then, I thought it was unfair and double standard-ish. I was not allowed to do what my brothers did. For example, my brothers brought home Cs and Ds, but I could not bring home anything below a B. If I did, it was a whole problem. Even a B- was pushing it because it was too close to a C.

I can recall preparing for prom my junior year. My date was a senior who I was really cool with at school. I was scared to ask my parents if I could go with him to prom. They surprisingly said yes but wanted to meet him first. A week or two before prom, he came by the house to introduce himself. After the pleasantries and questions about his family, my mama threatened to cut him up. My dad advised, if I was not brought home the same way I left, the young man would have a problem he didn't want. Very Martin Lawrence, Will Smith *Bad Boy*-like, but also totally serious. I wonder if he even remembers this conversation. All I could do was shake my head.

Luckily, they liked him and thought he was a respectable young man. We later went to prom and had a great time. My parents even extended my curfew, so I could attend an afterparty at the school. The school was literally two minutes down the street from my house. The trust had been restored between us. But I still made a conscious decision to wait until I got to college to start dating. If they acted like that with someone I was not dating, then who knows what it would be like with someone I did date! So it was a hard pass for me. I had to continue playing it safe.

***

My mom was the glue that held our household together. She was an old-school disciplinarian, a product of living with southern grandparents most of her childhood. She is a walking, talking, breathing miracle, and she birthed miracles. She experienced an upside-down uterus that was corrected prior to my and Lathan's conceptions. Doctors didn't expect her to have any more kids. Yet, she still birthed children who were destined. God had a purpose.

Her strength and tenacity are remarkable. I inherited my staying power from my mom. She has a grace to her and walks in muted regalness. My mom played no games, and her prayer life was (and is) a heavy blanket of security. I used to think she had a direct phone line to God. Because I was the only girl, she kept me protected and always had someone watching out for me. Although she was the shortest person in the house, you did not want to cross her. Unlike my dad, I was actually scared of her back then. But I was pretty much her shadow and went with her everywhere.

She had the prettiest, thickest hair with the softest skin. I would mess with the backs of her arms because they were so soft. That would aggravate her so badly. She taught me how to be respectful and maintain humility. She also taught me that everything does not warrant a response. Wisdom is my friend, and tactfulness is necessary. I finally mastered this in adulthood. She could make a K-Mart or Value City outfit look like a million bucks. She taught me how to hand stitch. She said I should know how to, at least, sew on a button and fix a seam or rip. I still keep a travel-size sewing kit on me.

She provided me with on-the-job training to become an administrator. Remember the pink "While You Were Out" note pads? If not, Google them for a chuckle. This was before cell phones and text messaging. She showed me how to correctly fill those out when she or my dad were not home. I would proudly sign the bottom and leave the note pile neatly stacked on the kitchen counter. She also taught me how to use a typewriter.

I would be her assistant, preparing for annual church conventions. Early on, she identified my neat penmanship and had me put those skills to use.

I mastered my "phone voice" while listening to her. Many could not tell us apart on the phone the older I got. From my perspective, those things came easy for her. She had always wanted to be a journalist or some kind of writer, but never got the chance. I inherited my love for reading and writing from her. She is creative by nature and loves to research. She can also sing a little and can hold down some soprano. She and my dad used to sing in a gospel group back in the eighties.

My mom knew how to cook chicken one-thousand ways. It was amazing to witness. She knew how to make a meal and a dollar stretch. The kitchen was her sanctuary, a place of peace and quiet. She would fuss at us if we forgot to pull something out the freezer as requested or if the kitchen wasn't clean.

When she got home, everyone was dismissed from the kitchen area. One of my favorite meals as a child was her fried chicken, baked macaroni and cheese, collard greens, and cornbread. And if it was in the budget, she'd throw in some candied sweet potatoes. She is an awesome baker and is known for her sweet potato pies and pound cakes. I remember her buying me my first Easy Bake Oven. I loved that thing, and it wouldn't take me long to go through the recipes. I couldn't wait until my parents bought me an extra set of recipes, especially after Lathan ate up my brownies.

My mom was always the first one up in the morning, getting things in order. I don't remember ever seeing her disheveled or unorganized. I didn't see this even if she was stressed or if there was a lot going on that day.

Saturday mornings were sacred. We could not make a lot of noise too early in the morning. This is why I value silence and quiet time on the weekend.

She made us clean up before we turned on the TV or left the house for anything. On Sunday mornings, I would wake up to her already showered, in her slip and housecoat, putting together something quick for breakfast. We had to have our clothes picked out and ironed the night before. There was no running around in a frenzy on Sundays.

During the week, we could not make a lot of noise because that was when my dad studied for a sermon. She would send us to our rooms, so he could concentrate. She taught us reverence and to respect his pastoral assignment. She was a stickler for being on time and being ready on time. If you were running behind, and your butt was not in that backseat once the car cranked up, she would leave you.

The *only* thing we did not get left for was church because not going to church was not an option. It was required. Other than that, she would make an example out of you.

***

My dad was the cool, laid-back parent who pretty much grew up on the streets of Boston. He was the good cop in the house. My dad has always been a giant of a man, standing at a smooth 6 feet 5 inches. I never found him intimidating or scary though. My classmates thought the opposite since he was so tall and looked like he could take you down with his huge hands. I can recall him disciplining me only one time as a child.

I refused to eat some nasty Rice-A-Roni he kept feeding us while my mom worked evenings. I guess he was over me and my attitude. In the middle of our family room, he lifted my whole body up by the collar of my shirt with one hand. I was up so high that I was eye level with the ceiling fan. He told me I was going to eat the rice and be grateful. That was the first and last time for me. He didn't spank me, but that was enough to scare me. *We good, Pops!* Funny thing is, he doesn't even remember this.

So it was either Rice-A-Roni or some seasonless, canned mixed veggies as the side item. You know, the corn, carrots, peas, and beans mix. The man wouldn't even drain the water from the can. He would just dump the contents of the can in a small pot and heat them up on the stove. No salt was added. Lord, help!

His other go-to was Hamburger Helper. Do not, and I repeat, do not *ever* offer me and my brothers Hamburger Helper. We will respectfully decline. However, his meat choices and breakfast items were always delicious. From his juicy, homemade hamburgers and fried chicken to his fluffy pancakes (with the crispy edges) and top-tier omelets.

My dad is also a visionary and is very intelligent. He's the type of intelligent that can complete the *New York Times* crossword puzzle in ink and answer the majority of *Jeopardy!* questions. I love to see his mind at work once he has an idea about something. He is a skilled woodworker and can pretty much build anything that involves wood. This includes closets, kitchen cabinets, bedroom and office furniture, frames, and even speaker podiums.

As a teenager, I was so excited when he built a dresser and chest of drawers for my bedroom. I still have memories of him working hard in our garage, day in and day out, with a large construction pencil tucked behind his ear. By the time he finished up, his nose hairs and clothes were full of sawdust.

Because he pretty much raised himself, my dad's perspectives were raw and different. Yet, they were also necessary. Sometimes, his sense of humor can be cringy from being a fireman for so many years. He coped with the intense nature of the job by keeping everything light-hearted. Even if it was something very serious. He explained this was necessary to keep from crying or going crazy.

He witnessed some gruesome scenes that most can only imagine or see in the movies. He shared one fire run with me that he has never forgotten. They were called to a scene where he saw four teenage kids burn up in the backseat of a car. They were around my and my brother's ages. They had gotten into a car accident and hit a gas line that exploded. My dad, then, had to turn around and go preach at church like nothing happened. He has never been able to shake that image and still can see their faces today.

My dad would dish life mantras such as *"They lie (referring to boys). Just keep on having birthdays. Women think in circles, and men think in straight lines."* These sayings make so much sense now. Each time we end a phone call, and after we say we love each other, he says, *"I'll talk back with-cha."* He taught me how to ride a bike, use a screwdriver, and mow the lawn with straight lines. The lines had to be straight. He taught me how to drive in a white, fifteen-passenger work van. This is why I still love big trucks and SUVs. He named this van Sweet Pea.

Sweet Pea had no seats in the back and would hold all his work tools. You had to sit on a bucket as a "backseat" passenger. Your feet had to be planted solidly, and you needed leg strength to keep from sliding back and forth as he hit a turn. Sweet Pea was also loud and puffed out a lot of smoke. You would always hear her coming down the street, and that thing could smoke a whole hog on a good day.

My dad is also a comical human being and a great storyteller. If you give my dad a mic, expect him to deliver a performance. He does not mind being in the spotlight. As a child, I loved to hear him preach. He would spin around in a huge circle when he got happy, pump his fists in the air, and yell out, "*Ain't God all right?!*" His robe would spin right along with him. His other favorite line was, "*Well, amen lights.*" This was when the church got quiet over a word that was tight but right. I would, sometimes, get called to sing a solo before he got up to preach.

He dressed in nice suits, and older pictures prove he was a lover of fashion. Lathan and I got it honestly. He even modeled for a short period of time as a young man.

***

My upbringing and my parents' influence and reputation impacted how I journeyed into adulthood. Even through the struggles, I had placed them on a pedestal. This is why it was tricky and isolating for me to navigate the stickiness of their separation and divorce. The life that I knew and how I thought it would turn out was shattered.

It was even harder to understand the relational pause with my father. I compared our spiritual beliefs to how I *thought* life *should have been* for us. Our lives and circumstances didn't always line up with what my parents' preached. It didn't even always line up with what I read in God's Word. We weren't supposed to live a life of struggle.

I buried a lot of the trauma and embarrassment as a way of survival. I coped with what my parents emulated. Oftentimes, I lost touch with the little girl who was fearless, who had the biggest faith. I often lost touch with the little girl who had dreamed big and sought refuge in that tiny space in her bedroom closet.

Little did I know how it would all boil to the surface. And little did I know how these experiences would positively shape who I am today. Each experience was not in vain. God had and still has a plan and purpose for it all.

# PART TWO: MY FATHER'S STORY

*"If we have built on the fragile cornerstones of human wisdom, pride, and conditional love, things may look good for a while, but a weak foundation causes collapse when storms hit."*
*~Charles Stanley*

THIS LIFE IS GHETTO.

*My dad, Lewis, at the scene of a fire at the Peacock Lounge on Auburn Avenue in 1985.*

# 2

## AN UNSTABLE FOUNDATION

*M*y life as a man was not built on a strong foundation. My family unit was untraditional. There was no family unity, and I pretty much grew up in dysfunction. My father was absent, and I never heard my mother tell me she loved me. If she did, I really don't remember. Our dynamic was strained at the most. I was a latchkey kid at four years old. My mother and grandmother lived together, and both worked during the day.

My grandmother cleaned houses, and my mom worked at a hospital. So when I got home from school, I was on my own. I basically lived in a house with two angry women. They each had their own anger issues and were like oil and water. They could not get along for five minutes and not argue. And I was stuck in the middle of this nonsense. I had a strong need for someone to just simply care about me.

My grandmother ended up with four kids and no husband. This was the source of some of her anger. She expected my uncle to be the man of the house after my grandfather ran off years prior. No one knows where he went. Tragically, my uncle later drowned at the age of fifteen in the Charles River.

As the oldest, my aunt had to step in and be the head of the family. My aunt had to go looking for my grandfather to get the alimony money to help take care of her siblings. This same aunt desired to go to New York to be a model years later. But my grandmother prevented her from going because she was expected to take care of the household.

My grandmother was no longer the maternal figure. She had checked all the way out for an entire year after my uncle died. So there was no love in the house. Only survival. It was a house full of secrets. And most of those secrets went to the grave with those who created and protected them.

My mother was twenty-five when I was born. She was not married to my father. He had just fought in WWII and went off to college afterward. The two met when they lived next door to each other. I did not have a relationship with my father until many years later as an adult. I don't remember his absence phasing me much then.

When I was nine years old, my mother married an old drunk sailor from Rhode Island. It was a train wreck. When he got drunk, he'd beat my mother. He smoked. And I hated him. They divorced after one year. Thank God. And that was the first and last time she got married. I didn't process the divorce one way or the other because my life had been so individualized. I had to be responsible at a very early age and had to care for myself. So their divorce didn't impact me directly. It was just another event I shrugged off or ignored.

*There were times when I wanted to talk with my mom. I would ask her about the things I saw and things that impacted me. I wanted closure, and I still had a lot of questions. Unfortunately, there were many moments when she didn't have an answer. Many times, she could not recall the situation, so I stopped asking. The older I got, the more I understood her response. There were many things I could not remember and still don't today. I blocked out so much trying to survive and to avoid the pain.*

*My brother was born when I was thirteen. His father was a married man with children. I never had a relationship with him, to say the least. Ironically, he was also a fireman. Contention grew between my mom and me over my brother. I was expected to be his guardian and caretaker while she worked evenings. I wasn't too keen on this responsibility. I wanted to run the streets. My mom had all kinds of things to say to me. She basically told me that, if I didn't like it, I could get out. So I did.*

*At age sixteen or seventeen, I packed my stuff up in a shopping bag and left. I had already dropped out of high school. I moved in with a friend for about six months. Then, my mom became apologetic and wanted me to move back home. But it was only to help her take care of my brother. I never returned.*

*I was eighteen when my girlfriend got pregnant with my first son, Damon. Everyone wanted us to get married. So I jumped in the service to escape the pressure of marriage. I couldn't even take care of myself. I knew I couldn't take care of a wife and a baby. And I had no place to stay. I joined the Air Force during Vietnam and left everything behind. And that's where I got my GED. I regretted that decision, but it was all I knew to do. I repeated what my father had done. I repeated what my grandfather had done. I ran away to avoid responsibility because I hated responsibility.*

*Responsibility had been imposed on me since I was that four-year-old latchkey kid. That's why I'm surprised Damon and I have the relationship we do now.*

*My experience in the Air Force ended up being one of trouble and drama. So much so, they put me out a year early, which was okay with me. In 1969, I was stationed in Montgomery, Alabama, when the Air Force honorably discharged me under general conditions. Their reasoning was that I was unadaptable to military service. But the real reason was post-traumatic stress disorder or PTSD. This was something I battled with until recently. I never was given help for it, and the memories were too painful to discuss. This is also the reason I receive disability from the VA.*

*After I was discharged, I knew I was not going back to Boston. I had visited Atlanta a few times while I was stationed in Montgomery, so Atlanta ended up being as good a place as any.*

*Photo taken when my dad entered the Air Force in 1966.*

\*\*\*

Over the span of my life, I ended up looking for love in all the wrong places. Because I came from a loveless environment, I had no concept of it. I had no point of reference for what real love looked like or felt like. I had no point of reference for what it would take to give love or even what it took to be loved. I was kind of void of that, so I made up my own scenario. I had to make up what I thought love was. And sadly, I really didn't care. I could give women a semblance of what love was. I talked a good game, and I had it down to a science.

After being discharged from the Air Force, I married my first wife a year later in 1970. We were married for six years. I only married her because of my mom. My mom was all in her feelings because we were shacking up during one of her visits, so I got married just to make my mom happy. Needless to say, it was not a healthy marriage.

She was all right until she got drunk and acted like a fool. I would hate to go to parties with her. She's the reason I slowed down my drinking. We would have knockdown, drag-out fights.

One day, she tried to run me over with a car at the fire station. She caught me out front, fogging up the windows with another lady. Then, you had the fellas standing at the window laughing at me, as I looked crazy, running away from her antics. They watched my ex-wife chase me around the fire ramp in a black Oldsmobile Cutlass, calling me all kinds of names. I couldn't really blame her though, but we could have resolved it in a more civilized manner.

When I got home the next morning, she was just as sweet and nice. I started sleeping with one eye open. She couldn't be trusted. Of course, the sweetness didn't last long.

She continued drinking, and I continued cheating.

At the church we attended, I had a woman in the choir. I had two others out in the audience, along with my ex-wife. I had no shame. For one of my birthdays, two of them came over to the house. They knew nothing about each other. My ex-wife offered to take one of them home after she got drunk. And that's how she found out about the other affairs.

Our relationship continued to decline. We were a mess, and we knew the marriage had run its course. After four years of marriage, we finally separated and divorced two years later.

\*\*\*

Ronnie was six years old when I married my ex-wife, Carol. I was just getting out of my first marriage. Our relationship and marriage started off rocky. After we got engaged, I messed up big time and cheated on her. I really wanted this relationship to be different, but I got hung up in the same vices. I didn't take enough time to get myself together before we started dating. I was still out in the world and didn't know

*God yet. So I broke off the engagement because of guilt. Then, we worked it out and got engaged again.*

*But by this time, my ex-wife had already formulated an opinion of me that wasn't positive. There was no trust. I don't think I ever fully earned it back. And I won't say that I didn't deserve this. She never believed me when I told her that I loved her. So after a while, I stopped saying it. I accepted defeat. I cheated and broke her trust. I also broke her heart, and I knew I had messed up. It was too late to undo it.*

*Lathan was born three years later. I had just come into the ministry and was ordained that same year. I had only been saved for a short amount of time. I didn't know anything. I didn't know anything about handling ministry life. I was still learning about God and how to be a Christian. I didn't know anything about how to be a good husband. On top of that, I was also still figuring out how to be a father.*

*Damon's mom was successfully raising him without me in another state. Yet, I thought I knew something. Even before my mom kicked me out the house as a teenager, I did not want any responsibilities. I rebelled against it. I knew I had to figure out how to handle responsibilities, but I did not want to figure out how to handle them. I had a passive aggression toward responsibilities. I would have lived on an island by myself if I could.*

*So, when my kids came along, and even once I married Ashley's mom, I could not give them everything I wanted to. I wanted to give them more of me, but I did not understand the responsibility of fatherhood at all. I did not understand the responsibility of being a companion* or a husband. I was winging it. I was like a duck in water. Cool as a cucumber on the top and paddling like a mad man underneath.

***

In 1982, our church sent me to pastor in Hogansville, Georgia, a small town located south of Atlanta. I knew nothing about this place. Just like everything else, I knew absolutely nothing about pastoring. I was still trying to figure out how to be a preacher. But the denomination figured they had a young minister, full of vitality, who could go save the ministry. We had five members. Three of them could not read or write. One was older than black pepper. Mind you, I was already struggling, and my finances were shot. Fortunately, the place we were renting only charged about five dollars a week.

On top of that, my ex-wife later became pregnant with Ashley. She was feeling some kind of way. There were still leftover residual emotions from when she was pregnant with Lathan. My mother had come to stay with us, and that was WWIII. Because of my tense relationship with my mother, their relationship didn't start off in the best way. I don't know what she was thinking, but my mother even rearranged our kitchen to her liking. Mind you, she was tall, and my ex-wife is short. This did not go over well. So add that on top of pregnancy hormones ... I almost lost my mind.

Now we're down in no man's land. She is pregnant with Ashley, and we still have no money. They expected me to literally build a church from the ground up, as if I knew what I was doing. All these dynamics were happening at once. I was a basket case.

When Ashley was born, I was fighting fires all night long to make ends meet. I would have to leave the firehouse and then drive down to Hogansville, about sixty miles down the road. So it typically would take me around an hour to get there. If you ever traveled down 85-South in the eighties, you know there was not much to see once you left the Atlanta airport area.

One night, I fell asleep at the wheel, and I literally ran off the road. When I woke up, I was running into a ditch. I mean, I almost killed myself going down there. There were times I had to cash out bottles just to get gas money to travel back and forth. There were many times I didn't have a dime in my pocket. It was a whole ordeal.

Most Sundays, I had folks staring at me like I was crazy. That wasn't encouraging. Then while I'm trying to preach, Lathan and Ronnie sat there looking like, Would you please hurry up, so we can get out of here? Ashley was the only bright spot because she didn't know any better. So I knew I had to make a decision. After a total of two years, I told the leaders I couldn't do it anymore. It just wasn't working.

***

Thankfully, I reconciled with my dad as an adult. Before he passed, being in his presence was priceless. The number of times we physically saw each other, in my lifetime, wouldn't even add up to a month. But *my dad and I had a good relationship. Oddly, I was actually closer to my dad than I was to my mother. We were so much alike, and our lives were parallel. We were two peas in a pod. The same things I was going through, he had already gone through. We thought the same. It didn't matter that I didn't grow up with him or that he wasn't around. I had no animosity toward him. I loved that man. I would gladly travel across the country for him if I could. I went to Phoenix one year to visit and didn't even know it was Mother's Day weekend. We went to church, and I realized it once it was announced. My mom and ex-wife were in Georgia. And there I was in Arizona with my father. Not a good look.*

*I can recall two distinct memories with my dad. One of those moments was when Damon graduated from high school. I flew in from Georgia, and my dad flew in from California. We sat my son down at the table that weekend. Because of the runaway legacy my dad had passed on to me, we told my son, "The buck stops here. This will not happen anymore."*

*We stopped that family curse and cut it off right there. As a result, my son did not follow in our footsteps. He didn't have outside kids. He got married in his thirties, had a son, and is a successful family man. He didn't run from responsibility like we had done.*

*Another distinct moment was the last time I saw my dad alive. His wife called to tell me he didn't have much longer. He was in the hospital dying of prostate cancer. It was eating away at his body.*

*While he lay there in the hospital bed, he was frail, and they had not shaved him. It really bothered me, so I asked the nurse to get me a razor. I prepped his face and gave my dad his last shave. The room was quiet. No one talked. It was just me and him. That was a moment I'll never forget.*

*Like I said, the number of times we physically saw each other didn't add up to one month. My mom would always tell me I was just like him. As I was shaving him, I noticed the hairs on his face grew the exact same way mine did. I couldn't believe it. The emotions I felt were unexpected because it was such a simple gesture. Yet, I didn't have a problem with any of it. That was the last time I saw my dad.*

***

*Even after reconciling with my father, I continued to struggle with my own fate as a father. I still struggled as a man. Life still didn't get any easier. It was one struggle after the next. I don't think I ever saw the light at the end of the tunnel. I was just merely existing. As usual.*

THIS LIFE IS GHETTO.

*Damon's high school graduation weekend in 1984.*

*Seated, left to right: My brother, Damon; my grandfather, James; and my father, Lewis. Photo taken by Lathan at six years old.*

# 3

## THE CONVERSATION STARTER

As he just shared, there are many things my dad does not remember. So some responses may appear lopsided as you continue reading. However, I am grateful he can share his vantage point to humanize his role as the "villain" of this saga. Not to be dramatic, but he's kind of always been the bad guy. And to some, he's still seen as one. I mean, you read the last chapter. The man was out here living carelessly and recklessly. But he is still walking evidence of God's grace. He is evidence of God's mercy and forgiveness. We both are. It was touch and go for a while, and I'm so glad we both lived to walk out this phase of reconciliation.

I see my dad as a man who never fully tapped into his potential or his position as a true king. There was always an internal and external battle that interrupted his footing. Sometimes, there was still a hint of shame he hid behind. That's why my prayer for him is that his latter years are better than his former. Our sit-down conversations have been refreshing. My dad has been able to lay everything on the table with such raw candor. He has shared the ugly and disappointing truths he could not express years ago. I appreciate learning his story from a clear-headed space and gaining his perspective on the decisions he made. I can connect the moments in time where I felt rejected to the moments in time where he felt dejected. These two spectrums were never disconnected.

My hope is that you capture the essence of his heart and transparency. Avoid judging his mistakes, so you don't miss the gems. In turn, my prayer is that you are able to see your own father, uncle, grandfather, brother, or husband in a different light. Men have a strong weight to carry, which most do silently.

As I forestated, some details may take you aback, surprise you, and make you rethink what you thought you knew.

Welcome to the conversation.

\*\*\*\*\*\*\*\*\*\*\*\*\*\*\*\*\*

## Ashley

My parents first separated when I was eighteen. The years leading up to their split were tumultuous and stressful. I really started seeing the decline after my dad retired from the fire department during my ninth-grade year. As I think about it, we were still catching our breath from my dad's exit from pastoring two years prior. There had been conflict between my dad and some of the bishops. I won't go into detail, but this resulted in a public and, somewhat, damaging blowup during the annual convocation or church conference. This was the time of year where pastors learned if they were reappointed or transferred to another church.

I remember it like it was yesterday. The church was uncomfortably silent. Questioning eyes glared at me as I kept my focus on my dad, who stood in the pulpit, my brother, who sat at the organ, and my mom, who sat in the front row. I could not wait to escape to the parking lot. My dad was angry, hurt, and justifiably humiliated. He chose to step down as the pastor of our home church after that. He had reached his limit. My mom's desire was to stay longer and fulfill her leadership duties until the following year. But my dad was ready to make his exit.

Life, as I knew it, was no more. For the first time, we did not have a church home. The inconsistency was brand new, unsettling and uncomfortable for me. I felt detached from relationships and friendships I had built since I was a little girl. From Sunday to Sunday, I did not know where we were going or if we were going to church at all. I was so used to being in church all day on Sundays. I didn't know how to handle having the free time. It didn't take me too long to adjust to that freedom though. I don't recall there ever being a family discussion or a kumbaya moment to reset. We were all just going with the flow.

My mom identified my struggle. She made it a point to create some stability for me. After a year and a half of a few ministry transitions, we landed at a church where we got plugged in and became active. Lathan had already moved out at this point and joined another ministry.

My dad retired when I was fifteen. Money got even tighter, and tensions grew. We would smile and interact with others at church, then disconnect and go to our separate rooms at home. Money issues led to stressful situations, which took a toll on our household. There were more audible arguments. There was a repossession. It seemed just about every other week or month something got cut off. Cut back on. Then cut off again. The water bill was the cheapest bill, and even that got cut off a few times. My parents would buy jugs of water from Publix for us to flush the toilet and boil water.

When the heat was off, we boiled water in a wok and huge pots, so we could bathe and wash dishes. It took five or six round trips up and down the steps to fill the bottom of the tub adequately. We rarely had cable for long periods of time, so the TV with an antenna and turn dial were clutch, even as technology advanced. I was happy when I finally got a remote-controlled TV with an attached VCR.

My dad would roll pennies, dimes, and quarters for gas money. Then, he would send me inside QuikTrip to pay, so he could avoid the embarrassment. I guess he thought there was less shame if he sent a child in to do it. I hated it.

I joined dreaded evening car rides to pay the landlord in Sandy Springs. These rides meant my parents were either at or beyond the grace period allowed for the rent. Thank God for *grace*. I would feel so bad for my parents and wished I had the means to give them the money they needed. I began to lock myself in my bedroom, trying to stay out of the way...until one day, when things sounded as though they were escalating outside my bedroom door.

The cause of the argument probably had to do with money. But I was ready to fight and defend my mother. Lathan had left an arm resistance exercise bar at the house. I grabbed it, prepared to put it to work. Now my father has never, ever put his hands on my mother. I want to make that clear. However, I was ready for whatever was about to go down.

I felt powerless yet empowered to intervene by any means necessary. Like many of you, I was taught to stay in a child's place and out of grown folks' business. But I felt God gave me an all-access hall pass on this one. You would have thought I was in an action movie with the James Bond soundtrack playing in the background. I was plotting and strategizing my next move. I even thought as far as what would happen if the cops were called. Luckily, I did not have to put that bar to use. I can't even tell you how the argument de-escalated. But it took awhile for me to emotionally recover.

\*\*\*

Even as the only girl, I don't remember being a daddy's girl growing up. But there was a block of time where we became closer once I entered my teen years. My mom was stressed out and did not talk much. I later understood she was focused on making sure I had the basic necessities. She borrowed when she could to ensure we had food to eat. Money was so tight leading up to me graduating from high school. Family, family friends, and her coworkers were our village. At one point, she worked part-time at Rich's (now known as Macy's) for me. So, of course, she was stressed. At the same time, my dad had checked out. I was going through the normal teenage woes. My mom and I were clashing regularly. We were like oil and water until I turned sixteen. We jokingly call those "the wonder years." *Y'all, that life was ghetto.*

My mom grew up in an era where children were not allowed to have an opinion and speaking up was considered talking back. And she had that black mama superpower of reading or hearing your inner thoughts. Even when you thought you were silently being slick. So I resorted to harboring my emotions and feelings to avoid losing my life and my front teeth.

But my dad was who I leaned on. He, sometimes, got stuck playing the peacemaker. He allowed me to actually speak, but I think he really just wanted the noise to stop. It probably was a flashback of him shutting out the drama between his mother and grandmother. Strangely, my dad has no recollection of this. He was unaware I valued him this way. He had mentally blocked out so much. Even the good memories.

## THIS LIFE IS GHETTO.

By the time I turned seventeen, my dad was like a stranger. I did not know who he had become. It felt like he was unable to separate what was going on in their marriage and his life, in order to just be my father. You'll read about it later, but he shared he had nothing left to give to anyone. We were not exempt. I understand his actions even more now.

During my junior or senior year, we had a snowstorm that came out of nowhere. It was enough where we needed to shovel the driveway in order to leave. This particular day, my mom and I had hair appointments. As we shoveled the driveway with brooms and dustpans, my dad remained on the couch, watching TV. He did not budge or even ask if we needed help. This was so out of character for him. I remember thinking, *Who is this man? What's going on with him?* A few months later, I unfortunately caught on to one of the reasons he was distracted. His infidelity.

This woman he was cheating with went to our church. I don't remember how I found out, but I do remember going through a range of emotions—shock, anger, disappointment, and confusion. I also felt so much pain for my mother. She never went into detail, but she knew what was going on. And there was much more going on behind the scenes. This other woman would boldly pull up in front of our house to either drop him off or pick him up. I was flabbergasted and disgusted by the blatant disrespect. I wanted to throw a brick or rocks at her car. Clearly, she knew my father was married.

Knowing my temperament at the time, I probably wanted to go tap on the driver's side window and introduce myself. 'Cause *she woke up and chose violence*. All I could do was shake my head when I saw her singing in the choir, standing a few rows down from my dad. Or when she innocently walked by the three of us at church. She could never make eye contact.

This was some stuff you'd see in a Lifetime movie. I couldn't believe this was playing out in my own home. Not my daddy. Not the preacher. Not the man of God. I never confronted him about any of the things I saw happening. I knew to stay silent. This was not the time to be nosey or ask questions.

All I knew was that my heart was broken for my mom. My heart broke realizing my home life was raggedy. Despite whatever issues they had and who was at fault, I felt my mom deserved better. Even my dad deserved better. I deserved better. We all deserved better. As expected, things kept getting worse. My dad became just a shell of a man who lived with us. That's all. Although he didn't intentionally do it, I felt he rejected me.

Looking back, my dad still made sure he was at the important events. If I didn't catch a ride with my best friend, he was the one who picked me up from after-school functions. He showed up to the senior meetings. He showed up to awards ceremonies. At my high school graduation, my dad was one proud man. He bragged on me and stood with his chest poked out as an adoring parent. But it was hard to see him full of admiration.

Where was this adoring parent while I pummeled through my final year, trying to graduate? Where was he when we needed money? Everyday essentials?

But he had been there. Just not how I thought he should have been *emotionally* and *financially*. I didn't account for the days he worked all night in the garage to finish up projects to bring in income. I didn't account for the days where he "robbed Peter to pay Paul." I didn't understand then what it took to be an adult. I judged from the outside. My dad also showed up in the best way he could *physically*. He had tried, whether or not he realized it.

Later that August, the time came to drop me off at Tuskegee. I was not sad, and no tears were shed. I needed a change of scenery. I needed the grounding of that tiny Alabama town. I was surprised my parents did not cry. My mom said, once she saw me comfortable and settled in, she was fine and no longer worried about me. I immediately made friends during orientation and was ready to start a new chapter. But life was getting ready to take yet another turn the following semester.

*******************

**LEWIS**

*For years, I was a shell of myself. I was still burned out from pastoring. I had nothing left. I had nothing to give my wife. I had nothing to give my children, the church. There was nothing. It started to come back once we later settled into a new ministry, but still, there were missing ingredients. We went through some emotional places up until that point. To build that back up, to make it look like something viable, was impossible. It didn't work out too well. So now, Ashley's mom and I had an even larger disconnect. And finances were not that good. Things got cut off just about every other week. I could never escape the feeling of drowning.*

*After retiring from the fire department, I was doing woodwork in our garage full-time. Ashley's mom was working part-time and doing real estate on the side. I'm at a point where I don't know what I don't know. I didn't know how things would work out. I'm working all I can. I'm out there busting my hump trying to keep up. Meanwhile, I'm still getting that glaring question from all sides: "What are you gonna do?"*

*I caught a lot of flack when I retired from the fire department. I don't regret my decision, but I missed what it provided me. I realized the fire department was a safe place for me. I had a place when I went into the fire house. I could block out all that I was having to deal with every day. I could go in and just fellowship with the guys, and we'd do what we do. I could decompress. But it all started back up when I cleared the sidewalk to come home. And then I had to deal with all the issues again.*

*My wood shop became a place where I could create and do what I needed to do rather than deal. So a lot of the things that I should have been doing with my kids, I didn't do. I couldn't. Number one, I didn't feel like I had the time to do it because I was so busy trying to make ends meet. Number two, I didn't have the money to do it. I'm sure the money didn't really matter compared to just spending time with them.*

*My kids have no idea about the guilt I felt. Even when they were younger, I felt so guilty because I was not able to provide them with the simple things. You know, just the simple stuff. I was not able to do that because I was so busy out there working. I didn't see what was important. I had gotten to a point where I felt my children really didn't like me because of what I had done or didn't do. I didn't feel like I was worthy of being loved by my kids. I felt like a failure and that I had let them down. To cope, I checked out. That's how I always coped when things got tough. I didn't know how to be honest with them. I wasn't good at having hard conversations. So I reluctantly accepted the failure.*

*Family life was still foreign to me. My ex-wife's family was so family-oriented, and there was always some sort of celebration or get-together. There was always something at her aunt's house. My mom lived about five minutes away from my ex-wife's aunt. For major holidays, we would spend about an hour at my mom's house, then go to the next stop. Or my mom's house would be the last stop. But I don't recall us ever spending a full holiday with her.*

*Holidays, such as Thanksgiving and Christmas, were never warm and fuzzy for me. Growing up, I cannot remember a major holiday where my entire family was all together. Even today, I still don't get excited about them. Holidays are just another day.*

*We would, sometimes, stop by Mom's after church, but never just to spend a long period of time. I sort of have myself to blame for that. Our relationship was still strained, and my family felt that energy. I didn't set a great tone. Thankfully, my sons had a very close relationship with her. The kids would often spend weekends with her. So while I was married, I still felt out of place. It was hard for me to fit in. My in-laws welcomed me, but it still wasn't enough.*

*Insecurities caused me to self-sabotage and prevented me from forming close relationships with them. I wasn't well-versed in family dynamics, so I accepted feeling like an outsider. Family was not a top priority because I was never close to my own. Family had not been a top priority for them either.*

*Luckily, me and my cousins are closer today and keep in contact. It was really hard for me to enjoy the moment then. Sometimes, I would opt out of showing up, even for my kids' birthday parties. I would stay home by myself and watch TV. But I regret I missed out on some important moments.*

# PART THREE: Our Story

*"A daughter needs a dad to be the standard against which she will judge all men."* ~Unknown

# 4

## THE SEPARATION

I will never forget the day I got the call from my mom in April 2002. She said, "Your dad moved out." Say what now? I distinctly remember looking at my dorm room phone as if I had heard my mom incorrectly. I probably did not blink much. I remember sitting, slumped over on the bed, feeling helpless, defeated, sad, disappointed, and confused. It felt like time had stopped until we hung up the phone. I wanted to be there for her at that moment.

My dad never called me. He never reached out to say he'd left. He never reached out to reassure me. He went ghost altogether. Consequently, that turned into almost two years of silence with about three or four interactions sprinkled in between. From my dad's perspective, I was unreachable because my mom and I were so close. He didn't know how to start the conversation. As I watched him maintain a relationship with my brothers, I felt rejected again. I asked Lathan why our dad was talking to him and not me. He didn't have an answer for me.

Then, Father's Day arrived. I was overwhelmed with grief and hurt. My mom had found another church home, and we went there that Sunday. It took everything in me to fight back tears and waves of sadness during the service. As I watched the pastor honor the fathers and beam with pride as a father himself, I sat back in my chair, feeling like an orphan. My mom had me speak with the pastor afterward. He willingly spoke life into me. He embraced me with a father's love and encouraged me to call my dad.

I mentally went back and forth, justifying why I should not call him. *Why do I have to be the bigger person? I'm the child. He left me. Not the other way around. There's nothing happy about this day. I know I'm required to forgive, but I don't want to.* After all, I was entitled to my anger. I managed to muster up some maturity and called my dad that evening, even though I wanted to sit in the middle of the floor and have a full-out tantrum. The struggle was real. I struggled to genuinely wish him a Happy Father's Day. I could tell he was shocked (yet relieved) to hear my voice. Needless to say, I kept that conversation short and sweet. That was my reasonable service.

My parents' separation also caused me to become more self-aware about how I dated. I started dating this young man my first semester of school before my dad left. We met the first week of classes, hit it off immediately, and became great friends. He was also my first boyfriend, so I was making it up as I went. Remember, I had told myself I was waiting until I went to college to date. I just wasn't expecting it to happen that quickly. But I was forced to face the very thing I had been evading — communication. All I knew was to hold things in, and I did not trust a lot of people. There was now an expectation for me to be affectionate, attentive, and nice. You name it. The basics. It was a challenge in the beginning. Communication with friends or family is different from communication with a significant other. My family and friends were accustomed to me shutting down or not talking. But you can only do that so many times with someone you're trying to get to know and date.

I gradually removed bricks from the top of the emotional wall I had built up for survival and safety. He effortlessly honored my deep appreciation for the small things and attentiveness. I used to have really bad cramps, and he bought me my first set of Thermacare patches. He dropped them off with a Snickers bar, a bottle of Coke, and an order of fresh-out-the-grease chicken fingers, with some honey mustard sauce on the side. Winning! It was such a simple gesture, and he did it without asking. It showed he paid attention. It was memorable because I didn't always feel fully seen up until that point.

He and his mom were also supportive during the separation. Our moms vibed right away, and they would regularly check on each other. Although we broke up near the end of our sophomore year, that planted the seed that I could have what I had not always seen. I was able to love and receive love from someone who loved me back.

I would often wish my dad was there to talk with me about navigating break-ups. I had others to help me through the process. I have a really close brother-friend in Memphis who I would talk to every day. But it wasn't the same as hearing my father's voice. I needed his affirmations. I needed his love and his big bear hugs. I needed him to tell me it would be okay and there were more out there. I mean, he was a walking playbook. I could've dodged some bad decisions later down the line.

\*\*\*

In 2004, during my junior year, I reached out to my dad to have a conversation. I had a lot of questions that were still festering. I wanted answers. Boy, was I in for a surprise. I was home from school, and we met at Applebee's. Once we got through the awkward pleasantries, I started firing away my list of questions. Lawyer skills on deck. "*Why did you leave the way you did? Why didn't you call to tell me? Why didn't you reach out to me? Why did you neglect me? Why did you neglect my mother? Why did you cheat on her?*"

To my dismay, my dad had no legitimate answers. At least, in my opinion. I don't even remember what he said. His reasoning was flawed, and his apologies were sorry.

I recall my dad just lowering his head in shame and defeat. He could not really articulate or form the words adequately. The conversation did not end well, and I left Applebee's more upset than I was when I arrived. For where he was at that time emotionally and spiritually, that's all he could really give me. But it was not good enough. I could not receive it. I was unable to show him love, even through the hurt. I missed the cues that he was reaching out the best way he could. I was unable to meet him where he was and show compassion. I selfishly felt his actions did not warrant it.

I did not formally date again until after I graduated from Tuskegee in 2005. Alternatively, it put me in a weird emotional space of learning what I should, could, and would tolerate. It also impacted my interactions with men. To some, I was an experiment to see if I was an undercover slut or an easy lay. Others wanted to know if I was as mean as most perceived. But it just took them getting to know me to realize I was cool and very down-to-earth.

All the while, I was battling to entrust my heart to another man. Even to people in general. I entertained some dudes long enough to prove a point. That they were not going to get sex from me. That there was a gem of an individual hidden within. You just had to authentically present yourself to discover it. Were they full of lies like my dad always said? Some were. Unfortunately, he had not explained the things to look out for. Just that *they lie*. I was able to figure out some things on my own. And you better believe I know it now.

My brothers never gave me a talk, outside of the infamous college-day chat Ronnie gave me. Their focus was on escaping home life and making it on their own. And rightfully so. And then there was the age gap. So I learned from them, and still do, by watching and listening. My ultimate goal was not to date someone like my father and get hurt like my mother. I still ended up doing both.

For instance, I allowed one to emotionally manipulate me. I watered down how God made me to keep the peace. I didn't water down God or His priority in my life. But I was not fully myself because it ruffled feathers, from the way I spoke to my perspectives and personal values.

As a result, he was more comfortable in his ego and avoided addressing his personal issues. I was adamant about changing the narrative of being the mean one. I didn't want to fall into the trap of chucking the deuces too early. So I tolerated more than I should have. I engaged in too many arguments. That relationship changed how I now handle disagreements and conflict.

I no longer raise my voice. I am intentional about conserving my energy and keeping my voice calm. I have friends and coworkers who say I have a therapist's voice. I will walk away from you or ignore you before you have me act a fool. *You ain't gone worry me* (bad English intentionally used for emphasis).

With another relationship, I lowered my standards and moral fortitude because the Christian ones turned out to be phonies. The ones who said they loved the Lord seemed to not know what they wanted. They frustrated me. So I said, "Let me try out those who were not in the church, per say."

I could be myself with them, and they didn't try to change who I was. They respected it. And they were not bad people at all. Thankfully, I also had some great relationships. They just didn't work out, and we were able to end the relationship on a good note. So I'm grateful for those experiences as well. But for some of them, I knew God wanted more from me. I just chose to ignore His expectations of me. I had the word of God in me, believed His promises, yet my actions and mindset were contradictory to what I knew. All because my heart was still rooted in unforgiveness and anger toward my earthly father. In turn, that unforgiveness and anger clouded my judgment. It also caused me to reject the love of my spiritual Father when I needed it most.

## Lewis

*I knew that, when I left the first time, Ashley was at a vulnerable stage. And to be honest, I was at a vulnerable stage, too. I personally did not feel loved or respected in my own house. As hard as I was working. As much as I was trying to keep things together. While having a conversation with my youngest son, I shared with him that nobody ever asked me, "How are you doing? Are you all right? What can I do to help you?" It was always, "Well, what are you gonna do?" So I was burned out. I had to apologize to Ashley for leaving her at the most critical time of her life. But I was mentally and emotionally out the door. I had checked all the way out.*

*It's March 12, 2002, my fifty-fifth birthday. Ashley's mom and I had about twenty-five years of marriage. And in those twenty-five years, we never really came to any kind of point of agreement. I mean, we pretty much stayed together for the kids. And I was miserable. She was miserable. Our never-ending cycle of financial issues didn't help either.*

*And at the time, I began to have a wandering eye. I was faithful to the marriage for about twenty-three years, but not the last two. I will be honest and tell you I was a boy dog out there. I was a player before I married Ashley's mom. When I came into the ministry, I left all that behind. I thought I had killed that monster. I thought I had done away with the need for other companionship. The dynamics of our marriage gave me an excuse to go somewhere else. Then, I could avoid responsibility. So the boy dog returned.*

*Just think of a recovering alcoholic. They can be sober for many years. But all it takes is one drink to set them back. Then, it all comes back. So women were my drug of choice. It didn't take but one time for the genie to come back out of the bottle. And I was out there again. No, I am not proud of it. I did it. I knew what I was doing, and I understood the consequences. Sadly, I did not care. I'm so sorry for my actions. Unfortunately, I was not sorry for my actions then.*

*So on my fifty-fifth birthday, I sat in our living room and realized, "Man, you deserve to be happy." And from that moment on until April, I was on my way out. I made the necessary preparations and got a place. I said, "I'm gone. I can't do this any longer."*

*I didn't consider how this decision would impact my family. Not even how it would affect my ex-wife at the time. My many years of unhappiness was the justification I needed. I had been running away from unhappiness since I was a kid. I know because my daughter saw the progression of the deterioration of our marriage, and me being gone probably didn't surprise her that much. Or it may have been just the suddenness of it. I don't know. But I didn't consider how my absence would hurt Ashley. Girls recover differently from boys, and that was very selfish of me.*

*But I needed a purpose. I needed stability. The bottom line is men need work. Women need security. If men don't work, women don't have* security. And if women don't have security, they can backlash. You're going to catch it one way or the other. So I was catching it big time. It's one thing to have to deal with nonsense and pressure out there in the streets. But you have to come back home and deal with even more pressure. I was struggling to provide for my family. I was working, but it was never enough. I felt like a failure as a man. I can't even describe what that's like. It's almost like I didn't want to go home. I'd rather stay out there than deal with everything. I needed an outlet.

As a result, I stayed in the shop a lot to escape the noise. Back in 1989, when Ashley was still young, my ex-wife's cousin was in the Navy and was stationed in San Francisco. He and his wife wanted me to drive their van from Atlanta to San Francisco (The Golden City). I was not working because I had hurt my knee. So I agreed and drove to California by myself. I stopped in Dallas and Phoenix, then drove to Los Angeles, where I saw my dad and stayed with him for a couple of days.

Once I got to San Francisco, I flew back to Atlanta. I will tell you it was the best trip I had ever taken by myself. Actually, beyond a doubt, that was the best trip I've ever taken. I was at peace. I mean, it was a long trip, but I was at peace. I didn't have to deal with anything or anyone except me.

***

*Once I left my ex-wife, I was literally a gypsy for a few years. I was between spots or staying with a girlfriend. There were many times I was homeless. I really had no direction. This is what my daughter saw. A father with no direction. I was in one-hundred percent survival mode. I was trying to figure out where I was going to sleep the next day. I had to figure out what I needed to do to make money for food for the week. But every Sunday, I sat up in the pulpit with my legs crossed.*

*I was still preaching and encouraging others while dying inside. No one knew I was living out of my car or the dirty lifestyle I had. On top of that, I had all this guilt weighing me down. I couldn't be honest with my daughter at that time. I was too ashamed to tell her I was shacking up with another woman. So when she had questions for me that day at Applebee's, I was unable to respond. During the separation, Lathan was open to me and didn't judge my low place. I could talk to him about the ugly stuff. So I was able to maintain contact with him. But I still felt like an outsider with all of my other children. I felt each of them were closer to their mothers, and I had no one on my side. I formed my own conclusions because of the shame and guilt, and that wasn't fair to them.*

*But I remember being so proud of my daughter while she was away at Tuskegee. She was doing so well and was active in school activities. I went to hear her give a speech for a contest, and she knocked it out the park. She even got a standing ovation. That was a great moment to witness. Then, she graduated from college, and that was another proud moment for me.*

*After she moved away to Ohio for law school, I really wish she would have finished. I was ready to see my daughter become a lawyer. But I wasn't privy to the circumstances surrounding that decision back then. I really thought I wouldn't see my baby girl anymore once she left Georgia. Our relationship was still a little strained, and I knew distance would only make it worse.*

# 5

## THE RECONCILIATION

After I graduated from Tuskegee in 2005, I went to Ohio for law school that fall. Surprisingly, my dad was the one who drove me up to Dayton. I did not have a car then, and no one else could take me. I called my dad, and he agreed to make it happen without hesitation. He got me settled in and immediately drove back the next morning to get back to work.

Throughout grad school, we managed to maintain a level of communication. Then, here comes something else. He was openly dating. I could not understand this because my parents were not divorced *on paper yet*. It had been about six years since he left my mom. Like, why are you two not divorced yet?

I'm not sure if he even thought to set that step in motion. He was active in church. He was back in the pulpit, and I was in full judgment mode. And I was just as wrong for judging him. I didn't have a heaven or hell to put him in.

He had come up one summer to visit after I moved into a new apartment. He was proudly updating me about his life and his new love interest. She had teenagers who were younger than me and my brothers. That felt weird. I felt he was trying to make up for lost time or opportunities with us. He explained how he had been involved in their lives and stepped in as a father figure for them. Go *figure*, sir.

I just sat back and listened, befuddled. I was confused about how he was taking an active role in someone else's kids' lives and not his own. I couldn't wrap my brain around that. But the kicker was, on the day he left to drive back home, he wanted to pray over my apartment and bless it. I was respectful and allowed him to do so. But I dodged him when he tried to pray over me and anoint my head. I hit a straight Matrix move. I wasn't confident in his salvation because of his lifestyle. I mean, I straight side-eyed him and his walk with Christ. He and my mom taught me not to let just anyone lay hands on me. So he was not an exception to that rule. Was I wrong? *Maybe*. Would I do that day differently? *Probably not*.

*\*\*\**

The summer after my second year of law school, I was put on academic probation. My grades had fallen below the minimum GPA allowed. I had not taken the time to really master how to study for law school. School had always come easy for me, but this was another beast. I stayed in the library during the week, but maintained a social life on the weekend. That strategy did not work. So this was my first taste of failure, and I didn't know how to handle it. I handled the stress silently.

## THIS LIFE IS GHETTO.

No one knew I was facing dismissal. I petitioned the board that summer and was permitted to return in the fall. I worked hard and got a tutor. I passed the course I had to retake but flunked another core class. I couldn't understand how that happened. I understood the material and was prepared, but my brain didn't process it correctly for the final. This time, I was permanently dismissed from school.

My plan A for life was shot. I had no plan B. Since the moment I gave up being a writer, I was going to be a lawyer and a juvenile court judge. So I guess I can say law was really my plan B after all. I sent out an email to family and friends to let them know there would be no graduation. I instructed them not to ask any questions and not to worry. But of course, they were worried and couldn't understand why I wasn't in school anymore. My mom definitely had a load of questions to fire off, but she refrained from doing so. I didn't want any sympathy or pity from anyone. I remember sitting Indian-style on my living room floor in disbelief and shame, asking for God's help.

On the day of graduation, I got dressed to go support my dear friend and my other classmates. I made it all the way to the parking lot but couldn't go in. I bawled my eyes out in the car. I felt so much guilt because I wanted to see my friend walk across the stage, but the shame, embarrassment, and grief were too much. I knew I wouldn't be able to stop crying, and I didn't want to ruin anyone's celebration. I took the entire morning to get myself together, so I could attend her graduation party later that afternoon.

After about a month of sulking, crying and worrying, I did what I do best and what my family does best — survive. I had been living off my refund check, so that held me over. I got a job at a law office and kept it moving. All the while, I really needed my dad. Deep down, I needed his affirmations and reassurance as a father. Thankfully, my friend's dad held me down like I was his own. He didn't know the extent of what was going on with me, but he helped to keep me alive. He helped me not lose my ever-loving mind. Still, I yearned for *my* father's love and affirmation.

That was the start of me making bad life decisions and bad financial decisions. I was in over my head, at times, because the money didn't always come in like I expected. Budgeting was foreign to me. Compared to my peers and others who had my education level, I was pretty much receiving minimum wage. I couldn't call home because my mom was still getting her footing, and I didn't want to bother anyone. I assumed my family was dealing with their own issues, and I didn't want to add to it. And I definitely wasn't going to call my dad. Pride got in the way big time.

Inevitably, just like my parents, I dodged a couple of eviction notices. Those late-night car rides with them to Sandy Springs became as real as ever. Fortunately, the front office was incredibly gracious to me. They prepared the paperwork out of formality but never filed it. Both times, they gave me an extended grace period to give me enough time to catch up. I am still grateful to them for being so nice and working with me because they could have been some jerks. But I'd had such a great track record up until that point, so they were willing to work with me. I contribute that to God really looking out for me and keeping me covered.

Also, like my parents, I experienced my own repossession. My lease was almost up, but I had fallen a few months behind. Yet again, I faced another failure I sought to avoid. I remember someone from the towing company banging on my door early one morning around 2:30. You would have thought I had drugs in the house the way he beat on my door. I packed up everything in large, black trash bags and watched him drive my car away. It was the first car I had gotten on my own. I then knew how my mom must have felt while watching our van get towed away a few years back. For about two months after that, I woke up out of my sleep every night at exactly 2:30, my heart beating out of control. The trauma was real.

For each instance I wanted to give up, God sent someone my way at the right place and the right time. And it was nothing but the hand of God and my friends' families in Ohio that kept me sane.

I then moved to Cincinnati a few months later. After losing my car, I needed to live closer to the new job I had gotten. Unfortunately, the bus system didn't travel that far, and there were no trains like in Atlanta. I took the bus to work every day for about eight or nine months. I remember walking in feet of snow to get to the bus stop on time. I would maintain my focus and stay grounded. And I did what I had always done — survived. I got really close to my riding mates because most of us took the same route and lived in the same area.

Later on, Ronnie bought another car and kept his '98 Nissan Maxima as a side car. One weekend, he let me drive it back, so I would have some transportation. He then offered to sell it to me, and he put me on a payment plan. I was surprised because he loved that car. And I fell in love with it, too. That car became my best friend, and I drove it until 2015 when I got another car. I took care of it like it was a Mercedes. It was at over

300,000 miles once I stopped driving it. I later sold it to my neighbor who needed another car for his household. I was glad I could pay it forward.

***

During the time I was still riding the bus, my mom called to inform me she had reconciled with my father. They were back together. *Slow blink*. Wherever I was at the time, I'm sure I was slumped over again in disbelief, like the day she called to tell me he'd left. *Good grief, Charlie Brown*. He had reached out to apologize to her for everything, and they had gone on a date. Understandably, I responded with a few questions, and she willingly answered a few.

But there was an opinion she would not entertain. Can you guess? My mom told me she did not owe me or my brothers an explanation and that it wasn't our business. Well, then. I'm not allowed to be concerned about this man who did you dirty only a few years prior? It was irrelevant that he was my father. He comes back with an apology and a hot meal, and now you're back on track? I had all the feels.

I vented to a few friends who were in disbelief as well. They thought I was making up the whole thing. I called my brothers for a logical response. They had nothing. We did not think it was a good idea, but we had no say so in the matter. It was not our business.

As with other times, my father and I never had a conversation about his return. I'm sure he didn't know how to tell me. It was weird coming back home to visit and seeing his things in the house, to see him hugging my mom again. That was foreign because he had been gone for about seven years. And I hadn't seen them happy for a while before that.

Nevertheless, it was good to see them reconnected and operating in ministry again like old times. Despite their issues, they were always a force together in ministry. Their gifts complemented each other well. My mom looked happy and not weighed down. My dad looked happy and content. Unfortunately, it wouldn't last long. But this was nothing new.

The Father's Day before I moved back to Georgia, I sent my dad a Father's Day card with a big old button to wear. And he did just that. He said he wore it to church proudly on his suit jacket. That was actually the first Father's Day, over a span of nine years, where it was easy to pick out a card for him. And I meant every word on the card.

Year after year, I struggled picking out a card because Hallmark and American Greetings could not capture the true sentiments of my heart. Even Mahogany didn't get it right. I just needed a simple *Happy Father's Day* without the warm and fuzzy because our relationship was not warm and fuzzy. So most of the time, I didn't get a card at all. But that year, I was able to find the perfect one. It was a long time coming.

*******************

## Lewis

*I came back the second time because God told me to. I'll never forget the day it happened. He put me in contact with Carol for a reason. It was to bring me to the point of forgiveness and accountability. I was thinking about everyone I had done wrong and those who had done me wrong. I was on my way back home, and I said, "God, if you want me to forgive, then you've got to take this unforgiveness from me." And as soon as I said "me," He took it away just like that (snaps fingers).*

*In the process, God woke me up one morning, and He had me call every woman I had done wrong. God had me ask for their forgiveness. I even had to ask my mama to forgive me, and she was no longer alive.*

*I, then, called Carol and asked her for forgiveness. I later went home and cried like a baby. After that call with my ex-wife, we reconnected, and that's when we started dating again. And it left many folks confused, including our children. A lot of people at the church were confused. They asked her if she was sure. Family even asked if she was sure. But we started back on good terms. I enjoyed us starting the dating process. We went out to eat and got to know each other again as older adults.*

*We went through a process before I moved back in with her. She was in a better financial position, and she had some clear expectations of me. Thankfully, I was in a healthier mental state than when I left the first time, but not where I wanted to be financially. In the beginning, we also identified we had some of the same quirks as before.*

*My driving still drove her nuts and raised her blood pressure. Earlier in our marriage, she would drive holes in the carpet with her heels. She had her own personal brake system in the passenger seat. Blame it on my days as a fireman. But she and I were in a good place for about three years after reconciling.*

# 6

## THE DIVORCE

In 2011, I returned to Georgia. I was empty in every area of my life — emotionally, spiritually, financially, and mentally. Life felt meaningless. I needed to return home for a fresh start.

One day at work, as I sat at my desk, I knew I needed a change. I literally felt like banging my head on the desk. I resigned from my job a few weeks later. Over the next couple of months, I packed up my apartment and put some things in storage. I left Ohio with $138 to my name.

In 2001, I left home broken and emotionally defeated. Yet, in 2011, I still returned broken and defeated in more ways. *Home* was now a different geographical location but with two different individuals than before. My parents were in a position to fully support and love me. Their focus was to see me get my footing again and to take a breather. But I rushed the process. It was hard doing nothing and processing my thoughts in the interim.

I started a new job within two months. I got active at church, and God revealed other gifts and talents I had buried or did not know existed. I became more settled in my identity without distraction. Yet I was hard on myself because I still felt like a failure. I had not fully forgiven myself for making bad decisions, nor did I give myself enough grace to grow as a woman. I still felt like a failure because I had not finished law school.

Many still didn't know the details around the situation. It had been three years at this point, and there was still a sting. I also was not able to accomplish everything I'd set out to do. One of my dreams was to move to either New York or Chicago and enjoy big city life.

I had said, many times, that I had no plans to move back to Georgia. This was a well-known fact. Well, life said something different. I had isolated myself from a lot of people, so I did not have to explain why I was back at ground zero. I'd isolated myself, so I did not have to fumble through articulating what was next, honestly, because I did not know. I was blindly trusting God at this point. Day by day. I did not want to explain why I wasn't a lawyer, why I was not married with kids yet, or why I didn't have my own place again. But I believed God had me and still had a plan. I overcame obstacles at work, and God afforded me opportunities to rebrand and position myself for promotions.

*Then, life got ghetto again.*

In 2013, I lost a very close friend from Ohio. She abruptly passed away the day after my thirtieth birthday. It was also one month before her wedding. I had no clue how to process that kind of grief. It's a pain I don't wish on anyone. I was used to experiencing death in the family because of aging or sickness. But I had never lost a friend before. The following year, I was promoted again at work, and that gave me a glimmer of hope.

Then, 2015 arrived and kicked my tail. That March, I lost another close friend from college in a fatal car accident. That was the breaking point for me. Both losses took an emotional toll, and I realized I didn't fully grieve the first loss. I felt like I was carrying a five-pound dumbbell in the middle of my chest. I felt so heavy, and my heart was heavy. I cried every single day for three months straight, putting my tear ducts into overdrive. I looked and felt like a hot mess. Only one person was honest enough to tell me I looked like I had been through hell.

I held everything inside as usual. It took about two months for the darkness and dryness to clear up under my eyes. It had gotten so bad I was peeling off layers of dry skin. I later tried counseling because I wanted help. I wanted to finally talk it out. Epic fail. I stopped going after two visits and chopped it up as a loss. The therapist wasn't my cup of tea. I wouldn't try therapy again until years later. I'd dealt with a few betrayals and was just sick of people. If it wasn't for my Ministers in Training class, I would have left the church and God. Accountability and staying in His Word kept me grounded.

Then, my parents' relationship started breaking down...again. They were no longer on great terms. They were barely speaking. That same madness had returned. They stopped sitting together at church. So awkward. My dad was sleeping on the couch and became aloof. Not just with my mom, but with me, too. He was showing similar signs like before when I was a teenager.

Then, in December of 2015, I watched him pack up and move his stuff out the house. I sat in the office that day, working remotely. His closet was in that room, and he didn't say a mumbling word. He moved silently, as if he was only packing for a vacation. He never said he and my mom were done.

All he said was, *"All right, baby girl, I'm gone. See you later."* He left his key on the kitchen counter, and that was it. I desired more than what I got. I desired a conversation. I was that eighteen-year-old again, piecing together my own assumptions. Instead of feeling helpless, sad, defeated, and disappointed when I *heard* about his first departure, I felt pure anger when I *saw* his final departure. The tables were now turned.

I was the one making the call to my mom this time. I told her my dad had left and moved out. She was neither surprised nor fazed. He had already let her know two weeks prior. That chapter was officially over.

****************

## Lewis

*I was so glad and relieved when Ashley moved back home. I didn't think she would ever move back to Georgia. It was good to have my baby girl back. Her mother and I had joined a young, thriving ministry the prior year. The church was new, and I loved the vibe. It was unusual and different. Those were good times, being a part of the beginning days. Going to this church was a blessing for me, and I enjoyed the ministry. I enjoyed the pastor's teachings. I enjoyed just being there in the environment.*

*Ashley's mom and I began traveling again for ministry. I got connected to a church down in South Georgia, and she would travel with me. I also became a part of a five-fold ministry program. This would be the fourth time I got ordained. Ashley's mom was able to witness me finish something without stopping. It was a long time coming and worth it. This process represented something much more. It represented a spiritual renewal. It represented me fulfilling a responsibility.*

*Our home church also allowed me to meet some really great men. We had a great fellowship, and we called ourselves the "OGs." Then, the young fellas began joining us. The comradery of the men helped me through some tough times. During our monthly sessions or weekly Bible studies, we were able to talk about things men generally don't* discuss. Things outside of just sports or work. We talked about some real personal stuff. Iron sharpens iron. And it worked for me.

I also met my new best friend during this time. We first met at a Good Year tire store. I was there getting an oil change, and he was there getting new tires. We sat in the waiting area and immediately struck up a conversation. We talked, and I witnessed to him. At the end of our conversation, I invited him to church. He had just gotten married, and he and his wife were looking for a church home. The rest is history.

We clicked right away, and it was cool. He was my best friend. I could talk to him about anything. It wasn't hard opening up to him. He passed away a few years ago, but the memories of our friendship will always stick with me.

***

My relationship with Ashley's mom began to shift again. From my perspective, Ashley almost served as a buffer between us. The seams started coming apart in our marriage. We couldn't see eye to eye, and we stopped communicating. We couldn't make it work. Because of the dynamics that preceded my leaving, we, somehow, both knew that it wasn't working on both of our parts. The marriage had run its course, and we were just roommates at that point.

We had made it another six years before ending the marriage for good. When I let her know I was leaving, she said she was surprised I'd stayed as long as I did. But I gave her a two-weeks' notice, and that was it.

*We never had a conversation after that, except to finalize the divorce papers.*

*Again, I didn't feel comfortable having a conversation with Ashley. I still didn't know what to say to her, and I didn't know how to say it. I didn't think she would be receptive to what I had to say, and I didn't think she cared. I know now that was not the case, but that was the mental state I was in.*

*Like before, I didn't really consider how my decision would impact my daughter or others, for that matter. To keep the peace and to stay out the way, I stayed silent. I didn't have my wood shop to escape to this time. I kept my head down, stacked my money, and prepared for my departure.*

# 1

## Damage of the Spoken and Unspoken

*"When she is quiet there is a reason. She is sorting through all the chaos in her head and all the madness in her heart"* ~LLK

\*\*\*

If you recall, my dad found it hard to disassociate his dynamic with my mom from his dynamic with me. I ended up doing the same thing, not once, but twice. I ostracized him after the separation, and I ostracized him after the divorce. I reciprocated what I had experienced. I, too, found it hard to disassociate my dynamic with him from the dynamic he had with my mom. There were times I could barely look him in the eye when I saw him. I was disappointed and expected more. I felt rejected by him both times because there wasn't a conversation. *The damage of the unspoken.*

As a man of God and minister of the gospel, I could only see through the lens and expectations of those roles or titles. My vantage point was blurred and unfairly judgmental. I still expected more out of him because he was the parent, my father. But I didn't give him the space and grace to make mistakes. I didn't afford him the space to be human and recover. To just *be*. It's crazy because I gave others more grace than I gave my father. I have always rooted for the underdog and will go to bat for them. But I failed to go to bat for my father when he needed it most.

What made matters worse was that some acquaintances, family, and church members had their own opinions as well. They couldn't disassociate the man from the act. Some would dump those opinions on me as if I asked for them. Sadly, some wished my father ill will and uttered negativity. Some said his life would be in shambles because he would no longer be covered by my mom's prayers. I think some genuinely were praying for my dad. But I know some were waiting for his demise. And some are still waiting on the sidelines to see him fail. But not on my watch.

They did not consider that he was still a father and a grandfather. I still needed my father. My brothers still needed our father. Regrettably, I allowed others to speak badly about my father, either indirectly or directly, to my face. PSA folks: Please stop doing this. Do not do it to children. Do not do it to adult children either. Many times, we do not realize our words have power.

During our conversation, I apologized to my dad for my actions and inaction. If you have also found yourself doing this, apologize to your parent(s).

Even better, bookmark this page. Put the book down and go do it now. No worries. The book will still be here.

***

Their words planted a bad seed. Their words fueled my justification to be angry with my father. Very few stopped to ask me how I was doing. They would ask my mom but would not talk with me directly. And opinions varied based on if it was a man or a woman. Men were more supportive and understanding of my dad's stance or decisions. They came off more neutral. Women were ready to stone him on my mother's behalf. At the end of the day, it was none of their business. Honestly, it wasn't my business either. The business and the tea belonged to my parents.

Regardless of how much I had seen or was directly impacted, it was not my relationship. My role was to love and to provide support from a child's place. It's possible I actually was not warranted a discussion with my father about when and why he left or even when he returned. Do I think it would have helped and prevented unnecessary emotions? Yes, indeed. But based on what my dad was dealing with, he still wouldn't have been able to give me the answers I yearned for. He was not in a healthy enough mental state to effectively communicate with me.

Some have even assumed I do not desire marriage because my parents' marriage did not work. I have never articulated that. That was and still is an assumption that some have made. I'm glad I did not rush into marriage. I also have been intentional about learning and determining what I want and do not want. I use these experiences and others' relationships to learn and to do better because now I know better.

There are some who assume I'm still not married because of my parents' divorce. Again, I never articulated that, and that's definitely not the case. Their journey is not my journey. I'm that one who will sit and act dumb when people talk *around* me as if I'm not in the room. I think it's very passive aggressive. If you answer on my behalf, I stay silent. If you choose not to ask me the questions to seek understanding, I will stay silent. This is a good thing and a bad thing. There were many things I could have nipped in the bud. At the time, I can't say that I really cared. I was tired of being overlooked and misunderstood.

***

But I no longer want to hear anything negative about what my dad did or said. I no longer want to focus on what he did or did not do. He has owned up to everything, and it is in the past. It took two to tango to get me here, and it also took two to get me to where I am. While my mom was the glue that held everything together, my dad was still the structure, the bottle that held the glue. While it has been hard for him to come to terms with it, his presence was necessary and had a positive impact. It was not all bad. He got some things right, even when he thought he had failed.

For many years, we chose to just focus on the bad. A lot of bad was happening, and we rarely had moments to just enjoy life or to be happy for long periods of time. *Life was ghetto and consistently life-ing.*

I often think of the struggles my dad faced while pastoring. He started that journey unprepared and unarmed with the proper tools. How would his life have been altered had he been set up for success? Or if he had reached out for help or felt safe enough to be vulnerable? During my master's program, my final research project focused on the increasing suicide rates among pastors. I interviewed a group of pastors across various denominations to gain their perspectives. I asked, why did they think pastors were hesitant to seek help when they felt overwhelmed?

There was a common trend in their responses: pride, ego, being exposed for not being capable of handling their responsibilities, and being forced to step down from self-made or man-made pedestals. Exposure breaks down this pedestal and leaves them vulnerable to face their authentic truth. They are left to face their struggles and any anxiety connected to the negative opinions of others.

Spiritual beliefs are, oftentimes, not enough to combat mental struggles. Their physical and emotional needs are, frequently, disregarded. And they are often not seen as humans who encounter human things just like everyone else. Just like my dad, they continue to suffer silently. Also, like my dad did, they ignored the signs that their physical and emotional health were failing. *The damage of the unspoken.*

When my dad saw those four teenagers burn up in the back of that car, he was afraid to show his vulnerability. He didn't want to expose that his heart was broken after watching those kids die. He didn't want to be judged or seen as less of a man for letting the tears fall. He needed to come home and cry in my mom's lap, but he didn't tell her what happened. He shook it off and acted like it was a normal day on the job. He kept the tears locked in, exacerbating the mental torment. All he could see were their faces flashing before his eyes. He drove to church, stood in the pulpit, and preached as if nothing happened. He did all of this while needing someone to preach and minister to him through the hurt.

So add these layers on top of just trying to be a man. My dad battled pastoring others and being responsible for their spiritual walk, even while some relentlessly sought to see him break under pressure. Some were intentional about making his and my mom's life hell. Thank God for the faithful members who supported and covered him and us as a family. My dad also struggled to pastor his own household due to guilt and inexperience. He was still that thirty-one-year-old man who felt he did not know anything. He was still the man who felt he didn't know anything about handling ministry life, who felt he didn't know anything about how to be a good husband or father. He seemed to always be in a tug-of-war with authority while trying to walk in his own God-given authority.

He bucked the system like he knew to do. Then, on top of that, he was still *silently* enduring PTSD from his time in the Air Force. My dad shared that PTSD manifests itself in many different and negative ways, especially if it goes untreated. Reading about its effects can only give you an inkling of what it is like to live with it. My dad's generation didn't talk about it, and many still don't want to talk about it. So imagine trying to combat flashbacks and severe anxiety and not be able to express that with anyone. *The damage of the unspoken.*

I chose to learn more about PTSD because it impacted someone close to me. I also wanted to research the signs and symptoms to help form an effective prayer strategy to combat its curses at the root. My dad hoped that what I learned about PTSD would help explain why he did some of the dumb things he did. He was coping. I'm grateful he is no longer just coping. My dad is free in his mind. My dad is free of the weight of trauma. We both have come into agreement that he will live out the rest of his days with a peaceful quality of life.

\*\*\*

I think my father needed to hear more often that he was doing well. When he aimed to do better, he didn't feel like it was enough. He also didn't know how to articulate that he didn't feel like he was enough. My dad needed to hear *I love you* more. He needed to hear *thank you* more. When these acts were done or shown, I think it was hard for him to receive it. He unknowingly rejected positivity and love because he was in a constant funk.

As he shared, he grew up void of love, so he made up his own scenario. He had to make up what he thought love was or what love should look like. So when the family and others did show love to him, he was unable to receive it. Love was foreign.

My father had seen too much without an explanation. There wasn't a resolve. Silence, avoiding responsibility, and burying trauma were his defense mechanisms. It's easier to block out the noise and trauma, so you don't have to remember. I, too, had seen too much without an explanation or a resolution.

Communication was not a common practice in my family. We swept things under the rug and kept it moving. As my dad had done, I used silence as a defense mechanism and as protection. I buried the trauma, so I could survive and not buckle under pressure. Fortunately, I have always tackled responsibility because I saw my mom do it, and it was my life to figure out. But there were many things I had not remembered or thought of until I wrote this book. I truly had to sit in the hard stuff and situations that caused embarrassment or shame. I had to be willing to open up. It was even tough to share some things with you.

Oftentimes, the damage of the spoken far outweighed the beauty of what was unspoken. There was wisdom in the unspoken. And there still is. There was clarity in the unspoken. And there still is. There were life lessons hidden in the unspoken. This still holds true.

There were perspectives in the unspoken. That's why I am so grateful that more conversations are happening now. The healing is taking place.

# 8

## COLLATERAL DAMAGE

As a result of my journey, I have experienced some collateral damage along the way. I may not have been the intended target, but I got hit a few times. Life has resulted in some scars. The effects of the spoken caused some collateral damage. And the effects of the unspoken caused some collateral damage, as well.

Some say a girl will marry or date some version of her dad. *Did that also hold true for me?*

\*\*\*

Back then, I was determined to not date or marry someone like my father. Yet, I still ended up dating or was attracted to men who had some of my father's traits. Both good and bad. My dad is great with his hands and is a skilled woodworker. I am attracted to men who can fix things. My dad is comical. I'm attracted to men who can make me laugh. My dad is a "cool cat", and I love men who are laid back and confident without trying too hard. My dad is dark-skinned, and I love a chocolate man.

On the flip side, my dad *was* a cheater and a manipulator. As he has admitted, he knew how to talk a good game and had it down to a science. I can sniff out smooth talkers from a mile away. And cheating was one trait I detested but still experienced. The few times I was cheated on, I immediately ended the relationship. I saw what cheating did to my mother, so I preferred not to sign up for the hell that came with it. I saw it as disrespect and an unnecessary evil. And like most women, and probably as my mom did, I could tell when the shift happened.

With one relationship, I told him up front I would not have sex with him. I was adamant about it, and he was fine with it in the beginning. But he later was determined to make a liar out of me. When I wouldn't bend, he fulfilled his desires elsewhere. In the end, I guess we both lost. I found out about the cheating from other females. They gave me a heads up, so I wasn't out there looking dumb. It wasn't until I confronted him that he admitted to it. I will confess — my heart was crushed. I questioned the validity of our friendship, and the trust was definitely broken. I kept quiet about it because I felt ashamed. How could I allow that to happen to me? It took about a year for me and him to have an amicable conversation. I held a grudge toward him that entire time.

We sat down and talked about what happened, and he apologized. I forgave him and was able to let it go. In the same way I treated my dad, I didn't give him opportunities to apologize or to make his peace. I felt he didn't deserve it then. History repeated itself. I, again, found it hard to disassociate my dynamic with him from the relationship dynamic I had with my dad. His actions reminded me of the sting from my dad's actions. From that conversation, we both realized the foundation to our friendship held more value than the cheating. We laughed and joked around like old times. The love was still there. Memories of the pain didn't even matter anymore at that point. And they still don't.

I was in another relationship where I let my guard down and decided to have sex. My spiritual convictions were heavy, but I ignored them. I was in a season where I was tired of doing things the right way. In my opinion, life didn't seem to be better for me when I *did as a Christian should*.

Things were fine between us in the beginning. After a few months, I gave in to the convictions and no longer wanted to have sex. Let me tell you, the Holy Spirit will save your life if you allow Him. My ex later began to fulfill his desires elsewhere. Just like my other ex did. We were experiencing other issues, so the cheating added fuel to the fire. Oddly enough, I knew the cheating would happen, and I communicated this to him. He denied it. I can only guess he thought he could beat the stigma, but I was no fool. Once that door is opened, it's hard to close it back without some kind of repercussions.

I had a different reaction to that relationship ending. My heart didn't break the same way it did the first time. There was hurt, but there was no breaking. I didn't feel ashamed, but I still felt disrespected. Ironically, I even felt relieved. I finally had a reason to exit. There was a point in our relationship where I expected the worst. I knew cheating was inevitable. I saw the parallels between him and my father. I could pinpoint the signs, unlike before. I think I brought it to his attention.

I don't remember how it went down, but he immediately apologized. I also allowed him the space to explain himself. His justifications did not matter, but I let him get it out. That was important. His reasoning actually had nothing to do with me, but his own internal battles. I think he also struggled with what love should be or what it should look like. Just like my dad. I did not fully forgive like I thought because it took me a few years to let the resentment against him go.

Of course, as my dad always told me, lies were involved in each situation. *They lied* to me. But why did they feel the need to lie? One ex even wanted to be friends afterward. At the time, I couldn't wrap my mind around being friends with a liar and a cheater.

From what I had seen, things wouldn't end well. I had fought enough, and I had cried enough. Those were definitely relationships where I needed my dad. I needed my dad to affirm me. I needed his counsel and his listening ear. He has always had an open mind and never addresses anyone with judgment. I credit it to his unorthodox upbringing. My dad has seen a lot, so he's not surprised by a lot. That's what I needed in those seasons. No judgment. I needed a male perspective. He actually could have saved me from a lot of drama through his own personal experiences.

Because I was still angry at my dad then, pride wouldn't allow me to seek him out for advice. I'm not sure why I didn't reach out to my brothers. I probably was too ashamed to share with them what was going on. And I was probably too ashamed to admit I got played. But I know, even now, that my dad would have willingly offered me guidance and red flags to watch out for. Would I tolerate cheating now in the dating stage? The answer is still no. Would I tolerate cheating as a married woman? My first reaction is no. As it relates to marriage, I won't even mention that possibility over my union. There are different expectations and an oath with God that's involved.

***

In the end, for some of my relationships, there was a mixture of guilt and shame attached once they ended. With each one, I desired to get it right and not mirror what I'd seen in my parents' relationship. I wanted to make better choices. I was fortunate to also experience great relationships that ended on good terms. There was no love lost. Those relationships ended for various reasons, but I didn't leave them angry. I am even still friends with some. All in all, I desired to be a better woman and to not repeat prior mistakes. I had improved as a girlfriend and opened up more, but I acknowledged I still had some opportunities around communication.

If I was going through something personally, I would, sometimes, rely on my first instinct to retreat and become isolated. I didn't always feel like I could trust someone with my personal issues or problems. The moments when I was vulnerable, I would, sometimes, hear: *"I didn't think you would go through that."* It was said judgmentally at times, rather than in a comforting manner. That is one sure way for me to shut down and not share ever again. And they probably didn't mean any harm, but that's how I took it.

Even with platonic relationships, I don't fully open up to most because many proved they were unable to handle my vulnerabilities. I've known many of my friends for over twenty years, and those have stood the test of time and loyalty. If you can't handle a small slice of what I offer, then you definitely cannot handle all of me.

One friend has described my approach so accurately. She said I place people in different-sized Ziploc bags. I identify that people carry various levels of capacity as it relates to me. Some can only handle a snack size, and others can handle the two-gallon freezer bag.

So now that I have learned more about my father, I wonder if my exes dealt with the same issues. Did I provide a safe enough space for them to be vulnerable and open up? Which sized Ziploc bag did I really offer them? Did they ever feel inadequate? Were they winging it like my dad, like a duck on water, looking calm on the surface while paddling like a mad man underneath?

Some of them had their own father issues and were trying to break their own vicious cycles. I always dated great guys, even the ones who cheated. In retrospect, their actions and decisions didn't negate who they were as men. They were also trying to figure out life, even with the expectations I placed on them. I have more compassion and understanding for them now. I can even understand some of the decisions they made during our relationship, even though I didn't agree with them.

***

Also, as it relates to men, I have experienced many incidents where I needed my dad's approval. As a teenager, boys were not my priority, so his approval wasn't necessary. And since he had said that boys lied, why even ask? What were the chances he would actually approve anyway?

The boy would grow into a man who lied, similar to what he did. My dad grew into a man who lied but did not know how to articulate this to me. As a result, I never probed the subject. It probably had to do with the conscious decision I made back in high school to wait until college to date. I wasn't sure how my folks would react, and I played it safe in that area.

Today, I welcome the insight, wisdom, and experience from both of my parents. They have both walked the journey I desire. They have experienced some valleys and low places I can avoid. They can share their opinions from a wife and husband perspective, their regrets and even successes. But whenever I do bring a man to meet them, they will know it is serious and game time!

Outside of my mom, my brothers, and my best friend and her sisters meeting my first boyfriend, I have never brought a man around to meet my family. My mom was the one who met most of the men I dated or were casually seeing. She was the parent my friends knew. So whether they met my dad or not wasn't a deal breaker then. Although we were not on the best of terms, I still respected his position as my father. If anyone was to propose, they would have still been required to ask him for my hand in marriage. I respected authority, and he was still my father at the end of the day. I had no desire to introduce him to anyone until it got serious enough for marriage. There was one who came close, but we broke up before my dad could meet him.

Also during this time, I had even braced myself with the truth of my dad not being available, as in not being available to walk me down the aisle. I had already formed a lineup of replacements in my head. I honestly didn't know if he was going to make it long in life. On the outside looking in, my dad didn't seem to value life very much. So I, sometimes, braced myself for the worst. That wasn't a good thing, but that's my truth. I would often observe my friends' relationships with their dads, and I desired the same interactions, to have an active and present father around. I wanted my dad to dote on me and ensure I had everything I needed.

***

I acknowledge my family dynamic also has impacted my views and habits as a woman, a daughter, and a girlfriend. I come from a heavy matriarchal family unit. There's an innate desire to protect women at all costs. My childhood is filled with memories of sacrifices and acts of love from the women in my family.

Many of the male family figures I admired had passed away in my childhood or they lived out of state. For example, one of my mom's first cousins lives in Ohio, and we were really close when I lived up there. I wish my dad also had these types of relationships and memories. Outside of his father, there was not a large village of male elders my dad trusted to help keep him accountable.

On my dad's side, he is now the oldest living male. His father passed away in 2004.

He is considered the *elder* of his family. This is still quite alarming to him. There's a certain weight that comes with this acknowledgement. Growing up, I only had a relationship with my grandmother (his mom). I don't have memories of my grandfather or interacting with him, even after he and my dad reconciled.

As my dad shared, he did not come from or have a strong family unit. Understandably, he did not benefit from a healthy, male-dominated environment. He witnessed a household impacted by the absence of his grandfather and the death of his uncle. The patriarchal presence was missing. His male predecessors had abandoned their place of influence and authority, leaving the women to figure it out.

On my mom's maternal side, the women were always the leaders and kept the family afloat. My grandmother and many of her siblings were married, but my great-uncles passed away before I could really get to know them. From my perspective, my second and third cousins were my male references. I, sometimes, wish I was able to meet my great-grandparents. My mom speaks fondly of her grandfather, who was like a father to her, and she was very close to him.

On her paternal side, there was a strong patriarchal presence though. However, I did not meet many of them or see them a lot. My mom's parents were not married when she was born, and she primarily grew up around her mom's family in the south. Similarly to my dad, she became closer to her father as an adult. He passed away a month after I graduated from high school. I miss him a lot, and I am so grateful for the long-distance relationship we were able to forge. He was a wellspring of wisdom I wish I was able to pull from more as a young adult.

***

Life, retrospection, introspection, and a good therapist have helped me identify that I need to tangibly and verbally receive love. Even from my father. No longer am I the little girl who was content with the worst-case scenario. No longer am I the little girl who had grown accustomed to tough love.

One Thursday morning, I was driving down I-285 to go into the office. I was having some quiet time and God corrected me in such a way that got me together. I had to clutch my imaginary pearls. I was praying for someone struggling to receive acts of love from others. They were too hurt to really see it. God then told me that was the same way I had been treating Him as my heavenly Father.

Over the years, He had been trying to show me His love and meet me in my damaged areas. But unintentionally and subconsciously, I was rejecting His love through my actions and disposition.

I, sometimes, acted as if I didn't deserve His love or was unworthy of it. That was so silly. My heart's posture reflected the heart posture I had toward my dad. It was inconsistent and, oftentimes, predicated on his actions, rather than just on who he was. I emulated what I saw. And it all stemmed from the continuous feeling of being rejected by my earthly father. I did not accept the only way he knew how to love me at the time.

My dad's capacity was not my capacity. I judged him based on what I *thought* he should have been able to give rather than what he *could* give me. I, sometimes, felt God was not there when I went through hard times. He didn't feel close. That was never the case. He was just waiting on my return.

Over the years, I don't think I struggled with the concept of love. I knew what it was like to be loved. I saw what love could be. I was able to show love, but I, sometimes, forgot *all* that love was supposed to be. The Bible lays it out clearly. Love is patient, kind, not jealous, not boastful or proud; it's not demanding, it's not irritable, and it *keeps no record of wrong*; it *never gives up* or loses faith; it's always hopeful and *endures through every circumstance* (I Corinthians 13: 4-7 referenced, emphasis mine).

I have not always been patient or kind. My love has been demanding at times and has kept a record of wrong. There were times I gave up on my dad and didn't have much hope in our relationship. But at the core, I think our love for each other helped us *endure* through every circumstance. We just haven't always called it love.

***

After I released the anger, resentment, and unforgiveness, my father and I were able to rebuild our relationship. It was not going to happen until I made the decision to forgive. After he left both times, I did not make it easy for him to reconcile. He was forced to walk on eggshells around me.

This was totally wrong and unfair. The same thing I accused him of was the same thing I did to him. I rejected him.

Because of the traumatic memory of him leaving again, I was unable to separate that he was only leaving my mom, not me. I had taken on and internalized my mother's pain and hurt. So my defense mechanisms were a hodgepodge of emotions that did not all belong to me, which I ended up using against my father. We had the same issue of failing to disassociate our relationship from the divorce.

No, I did not like the way he left. It was totally natural to be disappointed and angry. But I shouldn't have allowed that to interfere with the healing of our relationship as a father and a daughter.

I noticed he would always overcompensate when we communicated. I could tell he just didn't know what to say or how to even interact with me. I would say, *"Now, my dad knows I don't do extra. Please just be normal!"* But I failed to realize I was the thermostat to our interactions. He no longer knew what normal was. My dad couldn't identify whether I was hot or cold toward him. He just wanted to make it right with me.

One day, I asked God to heal my heart and remove the anger. I was so angry that it was no longer healthy. It actually had never been healthy, not even from the start. I was ministering to others about unforgiveness but didn't walk it out myself. I didn't want to see my dad overcompensate unnecessarily anymore. I asked God a few more times and left it at His feet to fix it. I knew it would only happen with His help. Because that thing was real. And He did just that. I do not know when it happened.

One day, I saw my dad, and all I felt was love and compassion. All it took was a decision and a made-up mind. That decision led to him being present when it counted the most.

Back in 2019, I unknowingly was battling severe anemia. For almost two years, I had been back and forth to the doctor with extreme migraines, joint pain, and swelling issues. Most days, I felt horrible, but I fought through. The doctors could not tell me anything or pinpoint the issue. The proof was in the blood tests the doctors never bothered to review. I had been anemic for over a year, but I didn't know how to read the test results. I thought my blood work was normal since the doctors never said anything.

One particular week, I had reached my tolerance threshold. That Thursday, I drove to urgent care after I left work. They ran a few tests and took some samples. My hemoglobin count was at a four, which is deathly low. The urgent care doctor sent me to the hospital to be admitted immediately. I was not going home. I was just a few days away from cardiac arrest. Because I didn't *look* how I *felt* and like what the numbers reflected, the doctor tested my blood a second time. Outside of my leg and foot swelling, she was in disbelief because I *looked* healthy, was still working full-time, and driving around like normal. It was nothing but God's keeping power.

I made the necessary calls, and my mom called my dad with the news. She and Ronnie came to the hospital, and my mom planned to stay overnight with me. As they were taking me out to place me into the ambulance, my dad was outside waiting with a load of worry on his face. I could tell he didn't know what to say or do. But he knew he had to show up. When I tell you that man trailed the ambulance as close as he could the entire way.

He literally rode the back bumper of the ambulance. I think he even ran a few red lights, so he could keep up. *For the entire ride, I kept my eyes on my father.*

As I laid on that gurney, filled with uncertainty, seeing the two headlights of his vehicle provided me a level of comfort. He was my focus. Once we arrived, my dad stayed until my room was ready. We waited for almost two hours, and the three of us were exhausted. The nurses then started preparing me for the first round of blood transfusions. By Friday evening, I was ready to go home.

A few months later, when I had an outpatient procedure, my dad was right there. He sat with my mom in the waiting area until I was moved to recovery. And he was my taxi ride home. Then, here comes another scare.

Two weeks later, I was rushed to the ER due to severe hemorrhaging. This time, as I laid on the gurney in that ambulance, *I kept my eyes on my spiritual Father* and sang and hummed myself to a place of peace. That was the most traumatic health scare I have ever experienced. I literally watched and felt life leave my body. And my dad showed up again and met me at the hospital. He was right there, and his presence meant the world to me. I needed him there, although there was nothing he could do but pray. As tears flooded my face from pure exhaustion, my parents sat together, side by side, in solidarity until I was released.

\*\*\*

All the life experiences shared in this book have directly and indirectly influenced my expectations of marriage. I have always desired marriage, but there have been times when I have doubted whether it would happen. I didn't want to always be the baby sister, or "last man standing", without a mate and kids. My sisters-in-law have already shared that I need to be the one to have the girl. *We'll see what happens, sisters!* What I have discovered is God still needed me to release myself from underlying resentment and unforgiveness. He knew I didn't need to carry those into another relationship.

God is requiring me to do things differently. I was holding on to a lot that wasn't healthy. There were some areas I had skipped over and never thought to revisit. The buried areas had festered. There are also times where I have felt behind the curve. It can be disheartening to watch your peers and classmates get married and have kids. But it's been even more disheartening to see some of these same relationships end in divorce. Some of them are not happy behind closed doors. The grass is not always greener. As Lathan says, "The grass is greener until you have to mow it."

But I desire to be whole, healed, and assured as a woman before I become someone's wife and someone's mother. I can proudly say that I am whole, healed, and assured. Everything I desire will happen for me, and the timing will be perfect. I can only attract God's best. Nothing can take away the invaluable lessons I have gathered as a result of this thing called life. Ghetto and all. I still survived. I still came out better, wiser, and more sharpened.

***

In a nutshell, everything comes back to the foundation. Not just for me, but for you, too. Our childhoods, our home lives, and our experiences shape our perspectives. It can shape how we respond to life's roller coaster. Our childhood plants seeds. We, sometimes, think our situations are so unique and isolated. But as you share more of your story and experiences, you'll realize that you are not alone. There are others just like you in the world.

My dad and I have many parallels. Some good and some not so good. But in his and my grandfather's words — *the buck stops here*. I don't have to carry what my parents carried. I don't have to learn the hard way in everything. I have the power to flip the script. Take it from me: Never forget to forgive. Don't hold grudges or hoard resentment in your heart. It will eventually rear its ugly head if you don't nip it in the bud. Life doesn't have to remain ghetto. It's up to you what you do with it.

Our choice to speak up cuts through the silence. Our choice to speak up invites forgiveness. Our story cuts through the insanity. My and my dad's testimonies have changed the family trajectory and welcomed more healing. Our testimonies have also invited healing into the hearts of others, just like you.

*The collateral damage was worth it.* There is beauty in the ashes. There is hope on the other side.

I am still that little girl who was fearless. I am still that little girl who had the biggest faith. I am still that little girl who dreamt big and sought refuge in that tiny space in her bedroom closet. I am still that little girl who never felt less than enough. I am more than enough. I now know how every experience positively shaped who I am today. It was not in vain.

You are a witness to God's plan and purpose for it all.

# PART FOUR: OUR HEALING CONTINUES

*"It only takes one voice, at the right pitch, to start an avalanche."*
*~ Dianna Hardy*

# 9

## WHAT WE SHOULD HAVE SAID

### To My DAUGHTER.

*I wish I would have dedicated more time to educating you on how to love a man. I emphasized that men lied, but I didn't emphasize why. I didn't emphasize who they truly are and what they need from a woman. We need a tender side from a woman, even while she's being strong. A lot of men will not admit this. But there will come a time when he will want to lay his head on his woman's bosom and just cry. He will want or need to be held by her. To find a safe place. To let him know "I got you, baby." Every man wants this from his woman. She doesn't even have to say anything. Just be present. Yes, we're all macho. But we're dying on the inside.*

*I wish I would have said I love you more than I did. I should have been able to do this, no matter what was going on between me and your mother. It was never my intention to hurt you. The toxic environment we created was not good for you or anyone else. But it wasn't about* you. It had nothing to do with you. It had nothing to do with your brothers. There were times when I did not even love myself.

Since I didn't grow up with love, it was hard to express love. I know I needed to tell you that more. I know I needed to do more things with just you or sit down and have a conversation. I don't know why, but I, sometimes, felt there was always an elephant in the room. I felt many were in your ear, whispering how terrible I was. I felt that prevented me from having a heart-to-heart with my daughter. I thought that, whatever I would have said, would have been negated by others' opinions and how I treated your mother.

Unfortunately, I was not in any spiritual, mental, or emotional position to father you and your brothers the right way. I was in a very fragile place, and I did not know how to deal with controversy. Even today, I still have problems facing conflict. I now realize you cannot have secrets. You have to make sure that, before you leave here, people know as much about you as possible. I'm hoping we can have more conversations. I'm hoping to have a better understanding of who we are now as father and daughter. We have a lot of gaps to <u>feel</u> and a lot of gaps to <u>fill</u>. And I know we'll get it done.

I love you, baby girl.

THIS LIFE IS GHETTO.

***

## To My FATHER.

Dad, I should have told you *I love you* more. I didn't *hear* it a lot, so it was hard to say it a lot. Expressing love and affection wasn't something exhibited in our family. Outward affection and love were foreign and awkward spaces for all of us. But I never doubted your love for me. I just didn't *feel* it all the time. I should have hugged you more, even when you didn't know how. I should have been kinder and more patient with my words, even in your silence. I should have listened to you more. I should have believed in you more, even when you didn't know how to believe in yourself.

I should have never given up hope. I should have been more compassionate when I saw the weight on your shoulders. I should have been more straightforward with you, even with the painful truth. We both needed the release. You were doing what you could in that moment. You did the best with the hand you were dealt. I should have honored you the same way I honored my mom. I should have forgiven you sooner than I did. I'm sorry for holding up the progress to mend our relationship.

I honor you. And, Dad, I love you. As you like to say, *you done good*.

# 10

## FORGIVENESS AND HEALING

*"And I will give you a new heart, and I will put a new spirit in you. I will take out your stony, stubborn heart and give you a tender, responsive heart."* ~Ezekiel 36:26 (NLT)

\*\*\*

Life can be ghetto out here, and we can actually benefit from the lessons it offers. We always have the option to conquer and overcome the ghetto-ness of it all. It's hard to share the past because of what our past represents, especially in Black families. It can represent shame, humiliation, abuse, guilt, and pain. You name it. It's hard to revisit the bad memories and dig up buried emotions and tragedies. There are traumatic experiences that should just stay buried and protected. But always ensure you are free from what the trauma represents. Again, never forget to forgive. Don't hold grudges or hoard resentment in your heart.

I encourage you to meet your parents where they are. Give them grace and understanding. Give them more love. I heard from a sermon that *nothing changes the inner world of a person more than love.* Love conquers all. Give yourself and your parents grace and understanding. You have to respect every decision they make, even if you do not agree.

To the fathers, whatever you're willing to share, please share. We need more. Daughters need more. More nurturing. More love. More hugs. More wisdom. More conversations. More context. Your story is not just for you; it's for others, too. Someone needs to hear your journey.

Daughters, I pray my journey assures you that you are not by yourself. Remember there is nothing like a daughter's love. Even if they cannot admit it, the way we tug at our fathers' heart strings can do major good or major damage. Please, responsibly water and nourish this gift. Our fathers need it.

Fathers, I pray my dad's journey helps you feel that you are also not alone. Transparency reminds us there's nothing new under the sun. Despite human expectation, God does not expect or require perfection. He's the only perfect one. He just wants *you*. He wants the flawed you. The timing of your healing depends on your reliance on God and admitting your flaws. If you do it in your strength, delays are always inevitable, and excuses will always hold you back.

In no way can I directly relate to the pressures my dad and mom endured together and individually. They did the best they could with what they had. They both did the best they could with what they knew. Now that I understand more of who my dad is as a *man*, it's easier to understand him better as a *father*. Who am I to keep reminding him how he messed up?

Facing his own guilt is enough salt on any wound. I choose to uplift and love him as much as I can now to help that wound heal for good. For years, it was hard to find a silver lining. I can truly say the silver lining is seeing each of us thrive in our own unique ways. Each of us survived. We kept fighting in our unique way. We have some bumps and bruises, but we survived. We failed at a few things, but we survived. Each of us has stability. We all have provision.

My family has an awesome testimony. I cannot fully articulate how proud I am of my brothers. All three were determined to change the narrative. They are now awesome men, husbands, and fathers. To see my brothers love and hug their sons and care for their wives is priceless. To witness my dad's restart and journey to better is priceless. To personally witness my mom in her right mind, retired, and spoiling her grandkids is priceless. It's a pretty big deal. And it's because of God's faithfulness and His mercy.

None of us were exempt from losing our minds. None of us were exempt from wanting to throw in the towel for good. It could have gone another way, but God's love and His grace kept each of us. Period.

\*\*\*

Just like my father and I, you, too, have permission to heal and to forgive. It all starts with a decision. A personal choice to forgive and to also request forgiveness. It does not start with an emotion. It does not start with how long you think you are justified to be or should be angry. Forgiveness does not require a ten-step process or a support group. Just do it. When you forgive, you give up feeling resentment or vengeful feelings against the *offender*.

If you feel any type of ill will or resentment when you see your father (or mother), you need to forgive now. If you feel any type of ill will or resentment when you hear their name or voice, you need to forgive now. If you rehash the past and the same hurtful memories over and over, you need to forgive now. Even if your father (or mother) has passed away, still forgive. Make a list of every last thing that is causing resentment and unforgiveness in your heart. Also include things you witnessed that indirectly impacted you. Then forgive them for each and every thing you listed and *release each one*. To release means "to escape from confinement and to set free." Release yourself from the confinement of bitterness and set yourself free. You can simply say, *"I forgive you,* **Dad (or Mom)***, for* **(what they did or said)**. *I let go of all resentment, hatred, and grudges. I break away from that hold and replace that space with love and freedom from the offense. I release you into the freedom of my forgiveness."*

Now do the same thing for yourself. Forgive yourself and release it. Do it as often as you need. Remember, forgiveness is not a one-time deal.

I acknowledge that some of your stories may be much worse and even more tragic than mine. I am aware and sensitive to that. Some of you have dealt with the loss of a parent, molestation, rape, physical and emotional abuse, displacement, abandonment, and even more. Some of you didn't get the chance to make it right or to hear the apology. Your parent may no longer be here. Some of you may have fathers (or mothers) who still refuse to apologize for their wrongdoings. They have too much pride or hate in their hearts. Pray that God fixes their heart because you can't do it in your own power. All in all, **forgiveness is still necessary. It is not for them. Forgiveness is for YOU.**

Forgiveness does not justify their actions or deny what they did to you. It does not mean you will forget everything you experienced. But forgiveness *releases you* from carrying the weight. You have to make a conscious decision to never pick it back up. You wouldn't want to dig back up useless, stinky trash, from a dumpster or landfill, to take back home with you as a guest or resident, would you? The same applies to unforgiveness and resentment. Do not dig it back up. Do not pick it back up. It all starts with a decision. It all starts with a choice.

*What's the worst that can happen if you let it go for good?*

\*\*\*\*\*\*\*\*\*\*\*\*\*\*\*\*\*

## Lewis

*As a man and a father, I pray that what I have shared about myself has helped you and opened your eyes. My hope is that my story can challenge fathers to an extraordinary journey toward forgiveness, peace, freedom, deliverance, and healing. This takes some vulnerability. I believe never has there been such a time as this when it is so incumbent upon men to fervently cry out to God. A cry that is heard in his home. A cry that is heard on his job. A cry that is heard in his neighborhood. A cry that is heard in his church. But, most of all, a cry that is heard in his heart.*

*First and foremost, before any petition can be rendered, there must absolutely be a cleansing of the heart. In Psalm 51:10, David asked God to "create in me a clean heart and renew the right spirit within me." The creative power of God is powerful. It's that same power that created the heavens and the earth. It's the same creative power that formed man from the dust of the earth. And it is the same power that can take the heart of a man and create something clean, pure, and loving without interfering with the true essence of who he is as a man.*

*In fact, this cleansing or purging has such a beneficial effect on a man. It makes him wonder why he did not allow God to do it sooner. The creative process that God uses can vary from man to man. But it is always the end result that counts. The end result is a man who loves God with all of his clean heart and is not ashamed to give Him all the praise for it.*

I cannot speak for most, but I am sure there are many other men who are just like I was: hard-hearted, stubborn, rebellious, unforgiving, and prideful. And like me, all while operating as a minister of the Gospel or in some other leadership capacity. Things had a way of being unfulfilled because of the excess baggage I chose to carry. But God's redemptive process is everlasting and well worth the journey. The process will also be worth it for you.

***

*"But when you are praying, first forgive anyone you are holding a grudge against, so that your Father in heaven will forgive your sins, too."*

*~ Mark 11:25 (NLT)*

***

*"And if he sins against you seven times in a day, and seven times in a day returns to you, saying, 'I repent,' you shall forgive him."*

*~ Luke 17:3-4 (NKJV)*

# 11

## A Letter to the Daughter

**To the DAUGHTER from a DAUGHTER.**

To the adult daughter experiencing daddy issues, you are not alone. To the adult daughter making a conscious effort to not relive the past, you are not alone. To the adult daughter juggling the complexities of her parents' divorce, you are not alone. To the adult daughter who sometimes feels stuck in the middle, you are still not alone. You are not by yourself. Focus on your growth and what's best for you.

Your parents' journey does not have to be your journey. You're allowed to make different decisions. And you should make different decisions. Don't allow people to speak negativity *over* you. Know that it's not your fault. As I like to say often, "You didn't ask to be here." But now that you're here, do your part. And live! It's so much easier to let things go that were and are out of your control.

I encourage you to try again. I charge you to forgive again. I encourage you to learn from every experience. Be honest about your feelings. Be honest about the void. Be honest about what frustrates you. Be honest about what violates your emotional boundaries. Lean into the love and security of your heavenly Father. Because He loves you, even if your earthly father does not or cannot love you like you need. You only get one mother, and you only get one father. Honor them. It is irrelevant whether you like them or not. It is irrelevant whether you agree with how they raised you. Still honor them. And that could mean honoring from afar.

Focus on who your father is as a man, instead of how he is as your father. They're connected but are two different things. Identify your father's context, his history, his insecurities, and his strengths. Then connect those to his role as your father. It makes a world of difference, and you will avoid unnecessary or selfish expectations he cannot or is unable to live up to in your eyes.

There are no do-overs, and life is too short. Forgive. Heal. And let it go. Do it as much as you need. I encourage you to seek help while doing so. Good therapy works. Find yourself a good "paid best friend." It hurt my heart to hear my dad say that he felt beat down because of the lack of trust and love. I never want him to experience that again. I've learned that men want to have a place where they feel significant and important. And that goes for our fathers, too.

# 12

## LETTERS TO THE FATHER

**TO THE FATHER FROM A DAUGHTER.**

To the father who has apologized, and your daughter still has not forgiven you, I accept the apology on your daughter's behalf. You are forgiven. To the father who has been too scared to apologize for fear of rejection, ask for forgiveness. Dismiss the fear and focus on your freedom. Release yourself from the guilt and mistakes.

If you have been rejected, be comforted in knowing you did your part to make it right. You messed up, but you still have another chance. As long as you're breathing, you have another chance. Pray and put it in God's hands. Please know you are loved.

As a man, you are worthy of love. Let no one convince you otherwise. You are not defined by your mistakes or what you were unable to do. I love you, and God loves you, too.

I want to share an excerpt from the book, *Crippled Kings*, written by Marquis Boone:

*"Yes. You were dropped! Yes. You were crippled! But today God picks you up. Not only does He pick you up but He restores you back to your position as a king. No longer will you look down on yourself and doubt and question your position because of what you have been through. You are a king and born to rule. No longer will you allow your mistakes of yesterday hold you hostage at gunpoint with the bullet of your thoughts. No longer will you sit and pretend to be perfect and secure as others struggle to be healed. At this very moment you rise. You rise and ascend back to your kingship."*

\*\*\*

## To the FATHER from a FATHER.

Before you can even think about being healed, you have to first ask God to show you the root cause. I facilitated a men's small group session a few years back. I learned that ninety percent of their problems were due to their relationship with their father. And that was an eye opener for me. So, for any man, I suggest you examine what your relationship is or was with your father. That will give you the basis for whatever healing will come from that. If you can't be honest about that, you will never heal. You will never be what you need to be. Most men do not understand or realize this. It took me a long time to get there.

A man is important in the household. He is essential, and God made it that way. Men have abandoned their oath. Many have abdicated their authority and their usefulness in the home. They've relegated it to the woman. So the woman has had to take on the part of being both male and female. And she's not equipped to take the man's role. I don't care how dominant she is. She's not equipped. Men have a dynamic that cannot be replaced. You have to first understand what your relationship *was* with your father and even what your relationship *is* with your father. Acknowledging this helps you come to a place of healing. Then, you can deal with it from there. Once you do that, you can start the process.

## OUR PARTING WORDS

**BABY GIRL** - *From the time you made your entrance into this world until now, I had no doubt that you would forever be my heart. Even in the times when I thought you really hated me, my love for you never wavered.*

*Taking into account all of the terrible and un-Christian-like things I was very guilty of, I never was too concerned about anyone else's opinion of me but yours. My main regret in the whole situation was that you and I never really sat down and had a talk with each other. Because of the overwhelming guilt I felt for leaving you when I did, I didn't feel worthy enough to be in your presence to try and explain myself.*

*I am so thankful to God for making it possible for us to have civil, insightful and loving conversations. And to have it put in a book is mind-blowing. No matter what has happened, what will happen, and what is happening now, you will ALWAYS be my loving, baby girl. Please know that I love you more each day, and I am so very proud of you and everything you stand for.*

*Love always,*

*Dad*

***

**Dad** - *It's amazing to see how far we have come. I am grateful to have you as a father. Thank you for helping me enter this world. Your seed has flourished beautifully. Dad, I see such greatness in you that you haven't even tapped into yet. You are royalty. You are a king. You are not forgotten. You are worthy of everything good coming your way. Stand tall, sir.*

*What you did and who you were in the past have been wiped clean. Whoever still tries to hold it over your head or throw it in your face, they can kick rocks barefoot. What matters is where you're going and the changes you've made. There is still more. God still has work for you to do. He still has people, especially men, you need to impact.*

*I pray you live out the rest of your days free of shame, guilt, and regrets. You shall live in abundance, good health, prosperity, and nobility. I'm grateful that God used this book to bring us even closer. I'm proud of you. Let's keep the conversation going.*

*May I continue to make you proud as a daughter.*

*I love you, old man,*

*Baby Girl*

# Acknowledgments

Thank you to my writing coach, E. Danielle Butler of EvyDani Books. Your direction, perspective, and push were necessary to see this to the finish line. We made it!

A huge thank you to my editor, Windy Goodloe with Nzadi Amistad Editing and Writing Services. You came in, tidied up the loose edges, and threw on some pretty wrapping paper with a big bow! Thank you so much for your eye and attention to detail.

Thank you to Dr. Tavis C. Taylor. Thank you for supporting my vision for this book. Thank you for incorporating your expertise, experience, and wisdom.

Thank you to each and every individual who endorsed this book. Thank you for your "yes" and for your support. Thank you for articulating your viewpoint and critique!

Thank you to my graphics and visual designer, Mike Danners of Iameye Photos. Thank you, thank you, thank you. You effortlessly brought life to my vision. You know what it is. Let's keep building together!

Thank you to my dear brother friend, James Artis Bogans III of The Artis Collective. Thank you for being the engineer and producer behind the audio version of this book!

Thank you to my mother and father. I love you both. As I've always promised, I got you covered when the wealth comes! Dad, thanks for agreeing to help me write this book. Your story is life-changing and necessary. Mama, your prayers were not in vain. May I always make you proud.

To my big brothers, I love each of you with my whole heart. Thank you for always being there and being great examples. To Carol Jr. and Kelli, y'all are the real MVPs. Hands down.

Thank you to my entire family for being a great support system and my personal cheerleaders. I am who I am because of my foundation. A special shout out to my dear Auntie Grandma, Robyn, Gregory Dan, Rory, Kenny, Lisa, Sherica, and the Rock of Ages church staff. You helped my mom ensure I did not go without during those tough years.

Thank you to Erica (Sissy), Adrianne (Bestie), Stephanie (my Ride aka Yvette), Dalita (DPipe), Kevin (Kevo), Tamira (Peterstj), Marquise (MG), James (JBOGANS) and Curnesia (Cora Mae) for your solid friendship and unwavering support. You have always believed in me and my greatness.

***

I must also publicly honor and acknowledge the parental village that has been my saving graces. God was very intentional and strategic in placing specific couples in my life throughout my adulthood because He saw the path ahead. The following helped change the trajectory of my life in ways they will never understand. They are part of the reasons why I was able to keep pushing when I wanted to tap out. I am forever grateful and I love you.

**HERMAN AND LATANJA HARRIS.** The parents of my best friend since tenth grade, Adrianne. Mr. Harris was always nice to me and just accepted that I was going to be at his house every week :) This was theeee only house where I could spend the night with someone from school. After my mom investigated and saw that you were good people, the rest was history. *Mama Harris*, you have always treated me like another daughter. Always. Thank you for allowing your home to be my safe space while in high school, especially when I needed to escape the craziness and stress of home life. Being the only girl and last child in the house, I didn't have anyone to connect with there. You never made me feel like I was imposing and welcomed me with open arms. During the school year and summers, riding with A, Kim, and Hillary to Gresham Elementary, where you taught, were some of my fondest memories. Thank you for everything, and I pray that you live the rest of your years in abundance and joy. You deserve it!

**WALTER AND THERESA GILSTRAP.** From our days at New Covenant, you took me under your wing and treated me like family. You never let me forget what God thought and said about me. You always spoke life into me. *Uncle Walt,* you were a fatherly voice and presence at a very vulnerable time. You and Pastor Bill were a listening ear as I faced those first few Father's Days after the separation. It was a lot to handle emotionally. You were always so easy to talk to and offered solid wisdom. *T Gran,* during those first three years of college when I wanted to give up and quit school, you gently talked me off the ledge and reminded me of the finish line each and every time. Thank you both for looking out for me, covering me, and making sure my mom was good while I was away at school.

**Isaac and Sandra Ivery.** My favorite landlords and the parents of my ride or die, Stephanie, whom I met at Tuskegee University in 2001. Thank you for loving me and literally treating me like blood family when I lived in Ohio. You allowed me to stay at your home for a few weeks while I was in between moves, waiting on my next check, and trying to figure out life quickly. I appreciate every holiday you shared with me when I couldn't afford to go home. Every Sunday dinner, every laugh, and every conversation. *Mr. Ray*, thank you for every lesson and for showing me how to change the oil in my car for the first time. You're quiet in how you move, but I learned a lot by just watching. And your humor is unmatched. *Mama San*, I've loved you since we first met in 2002. Thank you for your nurturing approach, for never judging me, for every "mama" gaze when you knew something was wrong, for praying over me, for your gentle spirit and patience, and for igniting an appreciation for gardening. I am forever indebted to you both and the Ivery/Thompson clan.

**Bester and Violetta Peterson.** The parents of my sister-friend Tamira, whom I met at the University of Dayton in 2005. I became the difficult, strong-willed child out of the bunch. But someone had to keep you on your toes! Since the first time I rode to church with Ma P and Tamira, and later that semester going to the house, you instantly loved on me. You fed me dinner and made me stay overnight, so I didn't drive back to my apartment as the snow built up. You got me through some very,

very rough times I told no one about. *Mr. P* aka my "*Rev. B. Lee Peterson of Dayton, Ohio,*" my mom had the nerve to give you parental rights and permission to act accordingly when necessary. You NEVER let me forget it. Ever…LOL! I remember my dad having a look of relief and peace when he met you because he knew I was in good hands. You have no idea how you saved my life, literally. You stepped in as an active father figure and never let me go without. *Ma P,* I appreciated and needed every hug, every smile, every pinch, every time you checked in when I isolated myself and checked out from everyone, and every moment of quality time. You and Mama San were my exposures to a real-life black Martha Stewart, and you put me to work. I'll forever ride with the Petersons.

**JAMES AND TERESA BOGANS.** I remember hearing about you before we even met. You (Mama T) and my mom had already discussed you adopting me as your daughter. How crazy! And now here we are. You two are definitely the hood/B-More version of my parents. When I first moved back, I didn't trust a lot of people, but our connection was easy. You all are a safe place where I can relax and just *be*. Who else would I watch back-to-back episodes of *Celebrity Family Feud* and *The Flintstones* with? Thanks for the late-night chats, words of advice, life talks, car rides, and inside jokes. *Mama T,* you kept me busy working at the church, keying in envelopes until I found a job. Those early days helped the uneasiness and feelings of inadequacy because I had no game plan. I just knew I needed to return home to reset and recover. We have a unique bond that cannot be broken. *Pops,* thank you for your humor, crazy personality, unbending stance, and being overprotective of me at the worst and best times. You're inappropriate when it counts, and you have the best heart. You are a living example of a man who goes hard and loves hard for his family. I love you both forever.

\*\*\*

*In closing, I acknowledge and honor my Lord and Savior, Jesus Christ. God, thank you for what's to come from this act of obedience. Thank you for the seeds of life that shall be planted within every reader. You knew and know the end and have been actively working behind the scenes on my behalf. Thank you for never leaving me. Thank you for never throwing me away. Thank you for still being mindful of me. Thank you for choosing me. I owe my life to You. I love You with all my heart, mind, soul, and strength.*

**"And we know that all things work together for good to those who love God, to those who are the called according to His purpose."**

**~Romans 8:28 (NKJV)**

# About the Authors

### Ashley R Wood

An intergenerational catalyst. A forgiveness revolutionary. A transparent conversationalist. Ashley R. Wood is the creator and founder of the *This Life is Ghetto.* series. Ashley has a passion for creating intentional and safe platforms for transformative encounters. Through real-life experiences and relational connections, her work is engaging and relatable with a touch of humor. Ashley co-authored her first book, *This Life is Ghetto: A Candid Conversation Between a Father and Adult Daughter Navigating Divorce and Daddy Issues*, with her father, Lewis E. Wood, sharing the full circle healing and repair of their relationship.

\*\*\*

### Lewis e Wood

A generational staple. A trustworthy source of wisdom. A healed reflection of redemption. Lewis E. Wood is no stranger to the peaks and valleys of life that can leave you breathless and defeated. He is a living testament to the transformative power of honesty, self-reflection and healing. A Boston, Mass. native, Lewis is a servant leader, husband, father, grandfather and great-grandfather. He is also a former pastor and retired fireman with the Atlanta Fire Department.

Printed in the USA
CPSIA information can be obtained
at www.ICGtesting.com
JSHW062048230524
63327JS00002B/2